Fast Feng Shui

also by Stephanie Roberts, from Lotus Pond Press:

Fast Feng Shui for Singles

Fast Feng Shui for Prosperity (coming fall, 2003)

Lotus Pond Press publications are available at quantity discounts for sales promotions, premiums, fund-raising, or educational use. Book excerpts and special editions can be created for specific needs.

for details, write to:
Special Markets, Lotus Pond Press,
415 Dairy Road, Suite E-144, Kahului, HI 96732-2398
fax your inquiry to (808) 891-0065
or visit www.lotuspondpress.com

FAST FENG SHUI

9 Simple Principles
for Transforming Your Life
by Energizing Your Home

STEPHANIE ROBERTS

LOTUS·POND·PRESS

published by Lotus Pond Press, 415 Dairy Road, Suite E-144, Kahului, HI, 96732
www.lotuspondpress.com

The author of this book does not dispense medical advice or prescribe the use of any technique as a form of treatment for physical, emotional, or medical problems. The author's intent is only to provide information of a general nature. It is the responsibility of the reader to obtain any appropriate or necessary medical advice or permissions. All recommendations are made without guarantee. The author and publisher disclaim any liability in connection with the use of this information, including but not limited to actions taken by the reader and the outcome of those actions.

Names and details in anecdotes have been changed to preserve client privacy.

Publisher's Cataloging-in-Publication Data
(provided by Quality Books, Inc.)

Roberts, Stephanie, 1958-
    Fast feng shui : 9 simple principles for transforming
    your life by energizing your home / Stephanie Roberts.
    -- 1st ed.
        p. cm.
        Includes index.
        LCCN: 2001116236
        ISBN: 1-931383-03-0
        1. Feng shui.   I. Title.

BF1779. F4R63 2001   133.3'337
                        QBI00-1078

printed in the United States of America

10   9   8   7   6   5   4   3   2

this book is dedicated to

JOHN
who introduced me to feng shui

&

TARAKA
who proved that it works

warm appreciation and thanks are due to

My feng shui teachers,
whose knowledge, insight and wisdom
enabled me to write this book

My clients, who are also my teachers

All my friends and colleagues,
whose advice and encouragement helped
shape and polish this book

and especially to

My wonderful parents,
Lloyd & Marge Roberts, for always sharing
your love and support no matter what
strange paths I wander

Mahalo nui loa to all of you!

Aloha,

It's hard to believe that not so long ago I was single and living in New York City. Using the same feng shui principles you'll find in this book, I focused on my goals, rearranged my home, and transformed my life. Today I live on the beautiful island of Maui with my beloved—and it's all because of feng shui. I'm writing this book because I want your dreams to come true, too!

Fast Feng Shui is for all of my clients who told me, "I bought a feng shui book, but it was too complicated and I didn't know where to start." It provides exactly what you need to get you off to a quick and successful start, so you can discover that feng shui is easy, powerful, and fun!

While I call my approach "fast" feng shui, because it will help you get started easily and quickly, my true goal is to teach you to see and approach the world with feng shui eyes. The best possible outcome of reading this book is that you will fall in love with feng shui and make it an integral part of your life.

Balance, harmony, and a deep satisfaction with who you are and what you are doing with your life can be yours. *Fast Feng Shui* is a powerful and effective tool to help you get there.

Wishing you joy and success on your feng shui journey,

Stephanie R.

Contents

Quick Tips

Introduction

How Feng Shui Works

FENG SHUI (say "fung shway") is an ancient Chinese practice that aims to maximize the beneficial movement of *chi*—the life force present in all things—through a space.

Where *chi* is strong the land will be lush and fertile, nourished by a good balance of sunlight and water, and supporting abundant and healthy plants, birds and animals. Where *chi* is weak the land will be barren, water is scarce or stagnant, and plant and animal life suffers. Just as fresh air, clean water, and organic foods nourish our physical bodies, so does fresh, clean *chi* nourish our lives. When there is a smooth flow of beneficial *chi* throughout your home, your life will be easier. Without a nourishing flow of *chi*, your relationships, creativity, health, cash flow and career may suffer.

Feng shui means "wind and water." *Chi* wants to meander through your home like a gentle breeze or a winding stream. Where the flow of *chi* in your home is blocked or weak, it is like a pond choked with algae and fallen leaves. You may feel tired, depressed, unable to focus, hampered in your efforts to move forward in your life. Where *chi* flows too strongly, it is like a hurricane or flood. You may feel out of control, overly emotional, or anxious much of the time. Business, cash flow, and relationships feel unstable as you struggle to "keep your head above water" through what may seem like an endless string of bad luck.

Feng shui uses shapes, colors, textures, sound, light, symbolic imagery and the arrangement of your furniture to adjust the energy of your home. Positive influences are encouraged and enhanced, while negative factors are corrected. Just as acupuncture works by correcting the flow of *chi* through the human body, feng shui works by correcting the flow of *chi* through your home. This is why it is sometimes called "acupuncture for the home." The goal is to create an attractive, safe, and nurturing space in which you can live and work more comfortably and productively.

Experiencing Chi

Chi, like the subatomic element called the photon, has no weight, mass, or dimension, yet is the primary particle from which the universe is created. Invisible and mysterious, *chi* can be easier to experience than to describe:

1. Take a minute to relax. Just breathe. Focus your attention on the breath moving into and out of your body.

2. Rub your hands together vigorously for a few moments, until your palms feel warm, then hold your hands in front of you with your elbows by your side, palms facing each other about hip-width apart.

3. Relax your hands. Breathe.

4. Focus your attention on a point in the center of each palm, then slowly bring your hands together until your fingers almost touch. Imagine that you are squeezing a balloon between your palms.

5. Now slowly move your hands away from each other. Imagine you are stretching a large rubber band. Relax. Breathe.

6. Repeat this movement a few times. Experiment with varying the speed of your motion and the distance between your hands.

7. Keep your focus on a point in the center of each palm as you move your hands, until you feel the subtle sensation of squeezing a balloon and stretching a rubber band (this may take a minute or two; closing your eyes may help). You are feeling *chi*.

Some of you will be able to feel the *chi* between your hands quickly and strongly. For others, particularly those who are not yet accustomed to tuning in on the energetic level, this may not come easily. Relax, breathe, and let it happen. Stop if you become frustrated, and try again another day.

Traditional Chinese Feng Shui

Ancient feng shui masters had specific guidelines for choosing building sites, based on the size, shape, and proximity of mountains and rivers, trees, roads, streams, and so on. This is known today as the "Form" school of feng shui, as it is primarily concerned with the forms of the natural landscape around a site. The form school principles are the foundation of feng shui as it is practiced today.

Traditional Chinese feng shui evaluated beneficial and harmful energies on the site and in the structure, based on the year of construction and the orientation of the building. An elaborate chart of numbers was developed that maps how the "flying stars" influence the luck, health and prosperity of the occupants. Annual and monthly star cycles are also considered. This approach is known today as the "Compass" school of feng shui. While this method of feng shui can identify energetic influences that may otherwise go undetected, it is quite complex and best performed by an experienced practitioner.

Another drawback to the Compass approach is that you must know the exact year of construction for your home—and of any significant renovations or expansions—and be able to get an accurate compass reading. This is further complicated because the "facing direction" is not always the same as your front door, and if you live in an urban environment getting an accurate compass reading may be difficult or impossible. For these reasons, the compass method is simply not an option for some people.

Another compass-based approach to feng shui uses the orientation of the front door to define four auspicious and four inauspicious sectors in the house. Based on gender and year of birth, four lucky and four unlucky directions are also defined for each individual. Ideally, the front door of your house would be in an auspicious sector and the front of your stove would face a lucky direction. You would sit or lie in an auspicious sector, facing a lucky direction, while you work, eat, and sleep. Many feng shui publications today follow this method.

In ancient China, you would live in a home that was selected or built for you with these traditional feng shui factors in mind. Today, most of us live in a house or apartment we chose without knowing anything about feng shui. You may be told that you should be sleeping with your head pointing North, but in your home that might mean placing your bed in an awkward position that causes more feng shui problems than it solves. It is unlikely that you can move your stove without kitchen remodeling, and unless you have a large home with a choice of several bedrooms, you will sleep in whatever bedrom is available to you, not the one in the "best" sector. While it is certainly worth taking advantage of your lucky directions if you can, even feng shui masters who follow this practice caution that following the rules of good feng shui "form" are more important.

Fortunately, as feng shui has migrated to the West, a new, form-based approach has evolved that is easy for anyone to apply.

Contemporary Western Feng Shui

Contemporary Western feng shui focuses on creating a healthy flow of *chi* through a space. Blockages and other forms of negative (*sha*) *chi* are removed or neutralized in order to welcome opportunities and encourage progress. Imagery such as paintings, photographs, and art objects is chosen and placed to enhance and reinforce the client's intention. It addresses the need for a method that can be used where compass-based rules of placement are difficult or impossible to follow.

The most widely known is the "Black Sect" method introduced by Master Lin Yun; most of the other schools of feng shui that have evolved in the U.S. are variations on the Black Sect teachings. Black Sect feng shui and its contemporary variations are founded on traditional Form school teachings. The major difference is that the modern practice no longer uses a compass; the association of specific areas of the home with specific aspects of your life is based on position relative to the front door—the "mouth of *chi*."

Another key feature of contemporary feng shui is its strong emphasis on the power of your intention to shift the energy of your home and initiate significant changes in your life. This self-empowering aspect of contemporary feng shui is a key ingredient in its populariy, and a guiding principle of this book.

Fast Feng Shui

Fast Feng Shui^{tm} is my approach to teaching Contemporary Western feng shui. It is based on the Black Sect and form school teachings, and emphasizes the power of your intention to accelerate change. Fast Feng Shui grew out of requests from my clients, many of whom understood the basic tools of feng shui but didn't know where to start, or who were frustrated by feng shui books filled with information that didn't apply to their home or situation. Fast Feng Shui closely duplicates the steps I follow in a consultation: analyzing the layout of the home, diagnosing problems, and prescribing appropriate adjustments.

Fast Feng Shui is designed to help you get off to a quick start with contemporary feng shui. It focuses on adjustments you can make right away, without remodeling, and helps you target the areas of your home that will have the biggest impact on your key issues. This book assumes that you are already living in the space that you will be working on, so information about how to select a good site for new construction or what to look for if you are shopping for a home or apartment is not included here.

This book covers a wide range of typical feng shui situations in a practical sequence that makes it easy for you to focus your efforts on the areas of your home that will have the most direct impact on your key issues. The nine Fast Feng Shui Principles (outlined on the next page) guide you step-by-step through defining objectives, locating your Power Spots, targeting key maintenance and clutter issues, identifying and correcting typical feng shui problems, and enhancing key areas of your home.

The Fast Feng Shui Principles

1. KNOW WHAT YOU WANT

Principle 1 shows you how to prioritize your desires for change, define your goals and focus on the specific outcomes you intend to achieve.

2. LOCATE YOUR POWER SPOTS

Principle 2 explains how to identify your personal "power spots"—the areas of your home where feng shui changes will have the most impact on your key issues.

3. CREATE A PATH FOR CHI

Principle 3 focuses on specific ways you can welcome more positive *chi* into your home and direct it to your power spots.

4. REPAINT, REPAIR, RENEW

Principle 4 looks at how common maintenance issues affect the feng shui of your home. You'll learn specific problems to look out for, plus how and why to correct them.

5. CLEAN UP YOUR CLUTTER

Dirt and clutter are like glue that stops *chi* in its tracks and keeps it from nourishing your home. Principle 5 provides tips for identifying and dealing with specific forms of clutter.

6. NEUTRALIZE NEGATIVE INFLUENCES

Principle 6 teaches you about common forms of negative *chi* that may be lurking in your home, and shows you how to remove or counteract them.

7. ACTIVATE YOUR POWER SPOTS

In Principle 7, you learn how to go beyond corrections to activate and enhance your power spots for maximum impact.

8. WORK ON YOURSELF AS WELL AS YOUR HOME

Feng shui is most effective when you work on your inner space as well as on your outer environment. Principle 8 reviews some methods for balancing and enhancing your personal *chi*.

9. EVALUATE YOUR RESULTS

Principle 9 provides guidelines and reminders for evaluating the success of your feng shui adjustments and learning from the experience.

What to Expect from Feng Shui

Traditionally, feng shui is seen as one of five factors that influence a person's life. In addition to feng shui, the other factors are your:

- **Karma**: your destiny or fate; the big picture of your life—whether you were born rich or poor, healthy or disabled, the major challenges you face during your life

- **Luck**: your astrology; periods of good or bad fortune; the types of situations and opportunities that come your way

- **Education**: your formal education as well as things that you do to better yourself, including therapy

- **Actions**: the integrity of your conduct; doing good deeds; taking care of yourself

The impact of feng shui is strongest when the difficulties you are experiencing are caused by poor feng shui in the first place, rather than by your karma, astrology, or actions. When this is the case, removing or correcting the problem can have dramatic and powerful results.

It is important to understand that if your karma or your astrology indicates a difficult life or a challenging period in your life—or if you have created problems for yourself through lack of integrity or poor judgment—feng shui will not magically erase all your troubles. By correcting inauspicious *chi* and strengthening the appropriate areas of your home, however, feng shui can ease a bad situation. It will support your physical and emotional strength so that you can weather the storm of a difficult period more easily, and it can help you regain the perspective and insight necessary for getting your life back on track.

At the very least, you can expect to create a more comfortable and supportive home environment. Over time, this will result in reduced stress, more restful sleep and relaxation, and greater self-awareness. These in turn will enhance your overall physical, mental, and emotional health. You will see improvements in your energy, enthusiasm and ability to work and communicate productively with others—all of which will have a dramatic influence on your life in the long run.

Other possible effects of feng shui seem quite magical: social and professional contacts may increase; a new romantic relationship may materialize out of the blue; opportunities seem to crop up everywhere you look; cash flow can increase substantially—sometimes literally overnight.

The effects of feng shui can be sudden and dramatic, or they might be gradual and subtle. There is no way of predicting exactly what will manifest for you, when, or how. Approach feng shui as an adventure, and be open to the unanticipated outcome that ends up taking you exactly where you need to go.

Feng Shui as a Path for Personal Growth

One of the best ways to ensure success with feng shui is to approach it with the goal of enhancing your personal growth and development.

For example, many people come to feng shui in hope that it will cure their money or career problems or bring a new love relationship into their lives. Some of these people will be able to use simple feng shui techniques to remove negative influences or to shift stuck energy and quickly realize their dreams. For others, feng shui is not so easy, because as wonderful as feng shui is, it is not a substitute for therapy.

This may seem obvious to you, but I have had people call me up and say something like, "I have some difficult relationship issues I'm trying to work through. Can I do feng shui instead of therapy?" To which my response is "You *could*, but why would you want to when doing both would be so much more effective?"

If you have trouble sustaining a long-term relationship because of intimacy issues, for example, using feng shui to attract a new relationship may bring someone new into your life. And then there you will be, faced with the same old hang-ups. Or perhaps you are having money problems because you are a chronic over-spender. Using feng shui to enhance your cash flow may lead to increased income. But if you are shopping compulsively for emotional reasons, having more money isn't going to solve your underlying problem—it will just encourage you to spend more.

People who turn to feng shui looking for a quick fix for deep-rooted emotional problems often discover that feng shui brings them lots of opportunities to repeat their old patterns of behavior. If you are really committed to changing your life, on the other hand, feng shui can be a powerful ally on your journey of self-discovery and healing. In fact, if you are truly ready to take your life to the next level, feng shui is likely to bring you situations and opportunities that will help you overcome the challenges you most need to address in your quest for personal growth and fulfillment.

It is my deepest desire that everyone who reads this book will achieve life transformations beyond their wildest imaginings. I know from my own experience that this can happen! The best approach to feng shui is to keep your expectations high while remembering that feng shui is a tool, not a genie popping out of a vase to grant your every wish. Feng shui will work better for you, and you'll get results faster, if you don't expect it to be a magic cure-all and are willing to work on yourself as well as on your home. For those who are ready and willing to change, amazing results really are possible!

How to Use This Book

The Fast Feng Shui Principles provide a wealth of information in "Quick Tip" format. Each tip explains a common feng shui situation, tells you what to do about it, and gives specific suggestions for how to use visualization and affirmations to empower your feng shui adjustments. As you read through the book, evaluate each tip to see if it applies to your home or situation, and if it addresses a priority issue for you.

Each time you come to a tip that applies to you, flag that page with a Post-It® note. Then, go though all your flagged pages and choose nine top priorities. Use your intuition to help you decide where to start. Include "should do" tasks as well as the things you most want to do.

Keep in mind that it's a good idea to take care of maintenance and clutter issues before activating your power spots, or you might end up activating the problem rather than empowering the solution!

A few more words of advice:

- Keep your momentum going. If you can do a little feng shui every day, that's great. Otherwise, make a commitment to complete a few more tasks each weekend.

- Be flexible. You may want to reorganize your priority list once you begin seeing things from a feng shui perspective.

- Please don't make feng shui changes for your children—or anyone else—without their permission. Explain what you're doing, and help your children feng shui their own rooms if they express an interest. Let your kids and friends see how much fun you are having with feng shui; when they get excited about it share with them what you are learning.

Your Feng Shui
Tool Box

The Ba Gua Energy Map

The BA GUA (*ba*: eight; *gua*: area) is a map of the energetic world. It is traditionally shown as an octagon with eight sections surrounding a central area, the *tai chi*.

For practical use, we extend the corners of the *ba gua* to form a square, then divide it into nine equal sections.

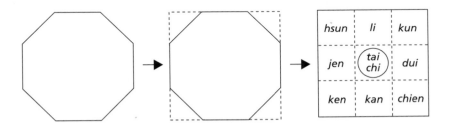

The *ba gua* divides any space into these nine areas. Each area corresponds to a different aspect of your life (coming up on the next page). Whatever is going on energetically—good or bad—in that part of your space will affect the related part of your life.

Every space has a *ba gua*. There is a *ba gua* for your plot of land, a *ba gua* for your house or apartment, and a *ba gua* for each room within your home. You can even apply the *ba gua* to your desk, bed, or stove.

The *ba gua* is rich with meanings and associations. The primary meanings of the *guas* are shown below. You do not need to learn the Chinese names, but they are a good reminder that each *gua* has many meanings. For example, it's easy to think of *hsun gua* as the "wealth" corner, but it is really about more than just money.

meanings of the *ba gua*

WEALTH (*hsun*)	FAME (*li*)	RELATIONSHIPS (*kun*)
Abundance Fortunate blessings Your ability to receive	Your reputation What you are famous (or infamous) for	Marriage Partnerships Everything feminine Your mother
FAMILY (*jen*)	HEALTH (*tai chi*)	CREATIVITY (*dui*)
New beginnings Your ability to initiate Health	Life balance (whatever happens here affects all *guas*)	Your children Your ability to complete things
SELF-UNDERSTANDING (*ken*)	CAREER (*kan*)	HELPFUL FRIENDS (*chien*)
Knowledge & learning Your spiritual life Self-awareness	Your life path Communication Social connections Wisdom	Benefactors/mentors Support systems Travel Your father

Placing the Ba Gua

To place this energy map on your land, align its bottom edge with the side of your property where the driveway meets the street. The street end of your driveway will be in self-understanding (*ken*), career (*kan*), or helpful friends (*chien*). Stretch the *ba gua* sideways and lengthwise to cover the entire property. It will probably end up as a rectangle rather than a square. That's okay. What *gua* is your house in?

To apply the *ba gua* to your home, align the bottom edge with the wall your front door is in. Even if you usually enter your home through the garage or a back or side door, always align the *ba gua* to the front door. Now, stretch (or shrink) the *ba gua* to cover your entire space.

To apply the *ba gua* to an individual room in your home, do the same thing: align the bottom edge of the *ba gua* with the doorway wall, and adjust the size to fit the space.

If there is more than one way to enter a space, orient the *ba gua* to whichever entry is most prominent. If neither entry is more prominent than the other, choose the one that is more frequently used.

The entry to any space will always be somewhere in *ken* (self understanding), *kan* (career), or *chien* (helpful friends) *guas*. As you stand in the doorway facing into the space, *hsun gua* (wealth) is always at the far left; *kun gua* (relationships) is always to the far right, and *li gua* (fame) is always at the center of the wall opposite you.

The *ba gua* for each floor above or below the main floor is aligned to where you enter that level from the top (for higher floors) or bottom (for lower floors) of the stairs. Sometimes there will be a wall directly in front of you at the top or bottom of the stairs, and you will need to turn to the right or left before you are facing into the space.

If a space has a recessed entry, align the *ba gua* with the doorway. As you stand facing into the space, parts of the room or building will be behind you. These areas will be extensions of *ken* (self understanding), *kan* (career), and/or *chien* (helpful friends) *guas*. You'll learn more about extensions in Principle 2: Locate Your Power Spots.

The Ba Gua and Compass Directions

Sometimes you will see the *ba gua* labeled with compass directions, with north at *kan* (career), and south at *li* (fame). In the Chinese system north is shown at the bottom, and south at the top, which is the opposite of how most of us in the West are accustomed to seeing maps.

This makes more sense when you understand that north is associated with winter, darkness, stillness, cold, and midnight, while south is associated with summer, brightness, movement, heat, and midday. When energy is cold and still, it settles; warm, active energy rises.

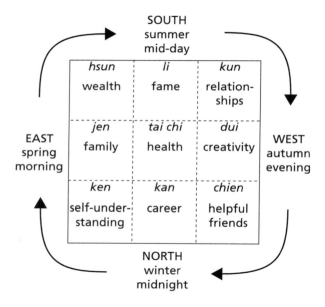

East is at the left side of the *ba gua*, associated with springtime, increasing light, warmth, growth, and morning. West, on the right, is associated with autumn, lessening light, cooling, decay, and twilight. Thus the *ba gua* describes the ever-changing, never-ending cycle of birth, growth, decay, death, and rebirth.

In traditional Chinese feng shui, the *ba gua* is aligned to the compass directions, and you may see it used that way in some books and magazines. This can be confusing, because in contemporary Western feng shui, the *ba gua* is always aligned with the entry to a space, so *hsun* (wealth) is always in the far left corner, *kun* (relationships) is always the far right corner, and *kan* (career) is in the center of the entry wall.

If you are concerned that by ignoring the compass directions you may be leaving something out, here's what I suggest you do. First, apply the *ba gua* to your home the front door method, and familiarize yourself with the location of key areas (wealth, relationships, etc.).

Then, look at the compass directions, and explore how the areas overlap.

DIRECTION	GUA	MEANING
North	*kan*	career, social connections
Northeast	*ken*	self-understanding, spirituality
East	*jen*	family, community, health
Southeast	*hsun*	wealth, fortunate blessings
South	*li*	fame, reputation
Southwest	*kun*	relationships, romance
West	*dui*	creativity, children
Northwest	*chien*	helpful friends, travel

Think of the compass direction as adding another layer of understanding to your *ba gua*. For example, if your *kun gua* (far right at back of house from the front door) is in the east, that's a great place for feng shui remedies to ease family tensions related to your love life.

You can use the compass directions as a tie-breaker if you can't decide which of two rooms to focus on. Or if the *gua* you want to work with is mostly in a closet or bathroom area, then check the compass directions as well to help identify other options.

Remember, if you find the compass directions confusing, or don't want to deal with another layer of detail, it's perfectly okay to leave them out. None of the suggestions or cures in this book rely on the compass. In Fast Feng Shui we are most concerned with creating a harmonious flow of *chi* through your space and with using the symbolic power of your imagery to support and enhance your progress.

The Five Elements

The FIVE ELEMENTS describe five qualities or "personalities" of *chi*. They are also called the five *transformations*. This is a better name for them because they have a powerful influence on what is going on energetically in your home. You can use them to enhance, control, or balance the *chi* of a specific space, depending on your needs. Since "elements" has become the most common name, that's what we use in this book. Keep the idea of transformation in mind, though, when you think about and work with the five elements:

- WOOD—the quality of upward growth, easy progress

- FIRE—the quality of excitement, expansion, quickness

- EARTH—the quality of settling down, becoming receptive

- METAL—the quality of contraction, sharpness, focus

- WATER—the quality of flowing, making connections

Each element can help shift your energy and/or the energy of your space. For example, use WOOD energy when you need to get a new project started. FIRE creates heat, passion and activity, and gets you noticed. EARTH is good when you need to slow down and relax. METAL helps you concentrate and get things done. WATER is helpful when things have been stuck for a while (think of ice melting), and for improving communication.

On the other hand, the wrong element at the wrong time can make a situation worse. When WOOD is too strong, you can turn into a workaholic, or become overbearing. If you're stressed out, more FIRE is the last thing you need. When you are depressed and lethargic, more EARTH will slow you down further. Too much METAL can give you a sharp tongue, and when you can't concentrate or make up your mind, it could be that too much WATER energy is making you "wishy-washy."

What Element are You?

Each of us has a unique combination of these elemental energies in our own personality. This affects the kinds of colors, shapes, and activities that you are naturally attracted to, and these can change over time. Probably you've gone through several favorite color phases in your life, perhaps loving green all through grade school, then discovering a passion for purple in college. Sometimes we aren't aware of the shift until a friend comments on it.

The element that is strongest in your personality right now will influence your current decorating style, housekeeping habits, and your approach to feng shui. Which one of the five descriptions below most closely describes you?

- NEAT FREAK: *I hate clutter! My home is immaculate, with everything tidy and well-maintained.*

- PACK RAT: *I can't get rid of anything. My house is so cluttered that when something is broken I can't even get to it to fix it.*

- FREE SPIRIT: *I'm too busy being me to clean up! If something's a mess, I just toss a shawl over it. People say my home has lots of personality.*

- GO-GETTER: *Housekeeping? Home décor? Don't ask me; that's what the maid and decorator are for.*

- WHIRLWIND: *Enough of the quiz already! I have a million things to do and a short attention span—just tell me how to feng shui my house!*

Many people are a combination of styles, so it may be hard to choose just one answer. If you're not sure, ask a few relatives or close friends for feedback; if you're a true Neat Freak, you may think your house is a mess even when it's immaculate by other people's standards!

Now, take another look at the information on page 20. Can you guess which feng shui style matches which element?

Neat Freak: *metal;* Pack Rat: *earth;* Free Spirit: *water;* Go-Getter: *wood;* Whirlwind: *fire*

Element Shapes and Colors

Each element is associated with specific shapes and colors:

- Wood—greens and light blues; tall narrow shapes

- Fire—reds, purples, bright oranges; triangles, flame shapes and other pointed or angular shapes

- Earth—browns, yellows, cool or muted oranges; low, flat, square shapes

- Metal—whites, gold, silver, grey; round and oval shapes, arches

- Water—black and dark blues; sinuous, curvy, irregular, and wave-like shapes

This is the basic information that you can use to adjust the energy of specific rooms and areas of your home. For example, to spice up your relationship areas, add more FIRE energy: things that are red, pink, and/or triangular in shape.

The material that something is made of is important, too. Some obvious examples are:

- Pottery bowl—EARTH

- Fish tank—WATER

- Electric lights—FIRE

- Houseplants and flowers—WOOD

- Brass clock—METAL

Others are not so obvious. A mahogany dining table, for example, is made out of wood, but it is square, flat, and (unless it's been painted) brown in color. In energetic terms, then, it has more EARTH energy than WOOD energy, because the wood is no longer vital and growing, and the shape and color of the table are associated with EARTH. A candle is a good example of the FIRE element, but if it is a tall green candle it also has WOOD energy because of its shape and color.

Many items have a combination of qualities, so you will need to use your best judgment about how much of what kind of influence it will have on your space. Try not to go nuts puzzling over what element something represents. If it's not clear right away, then chances are good it combines several different qualities and will not have as strong an impact on your space.

Keep in mind that function, placement, and your own intention are important, too (you'll learn more about these as we go along). If you worry so much about choosing the right elements that you no longer enjoy your possessions, you're trying too hard! Feng shui should be easy, graceful, and fun. If you love something, it has good *chi* for you. And once you identify your power spots (coming up soon!) you'll know just where to put it.

Element Cycles: How the Energies Interact

The five elements interact with each other in very specific ways. This enables you to be more sophisticated and flexible in your use of the elements as you feng shui your home. For example, to increase the FIRE energy in a space, you can feed it by adding WOOD. Too much FIRE going on? Add WATER to cool it down. Once you understand these different interactions, you'll always know what element to use where and why—so read on!

THE CREATIVE CYCLE

Each of the five elements is nourished, supported, or "fed" by one of the other elements. This forms a sequence called the Creative cycle (sometimes called the Productive cycle), as shown below.

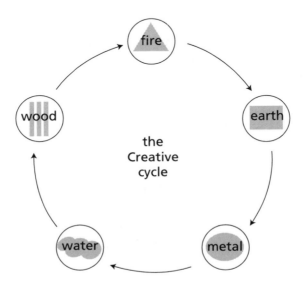

Here's how it works:

- WOOD feeds FIRE (without fuel, fire cannot burn)

- FIRE creates EARTH (as the fire burns, it produces a pile of ashes; think of a volcano becoming a mountain)

- EARTH produces METAL (metal is extracted from the earth)

- METAL produces WATER (think of moisture condensing on a cold can of soda on a hot day)

- WATER nourishes WOOD (without water, wood will die)

Use the Creative cycle when you want to increase the effect of an element in a particular space.

THE REDUCING CYCLE

As each element feeds or nourishes the next in the Creative cycle, its own energy is reduced by the effort. For example, you can counteract the strong WATER energy in a bathroom by adding WOOD energy to the space (green towels, for example). This gives the WATER something to do (feeding WOOD), reduces its strength, and helps bring things back into balance.

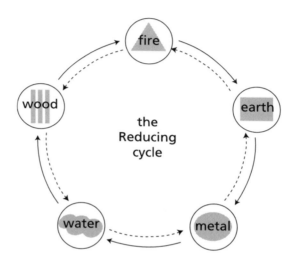

Here's how the Reducing cycle works:

- WOOD reduces WATER

- WATER reduces METAL

- METAL reduces EARTH

- EARTH reduces FIRE

- FIRE reduces WOOD

Use the Reducing cycle when you want a gentle way to bring a situation into better balance. It's easy to remember the Reducing cycle if you know the Creative cycle; just keep in mind that when one element nourishes another one, its own energy is reduced by the effort.

25

THE CONTROLLING CYCLE

When one element is very strong, you may need something stronger than the reducing effect to bring it back into balance. This is where the Controlling cycle comes in handy. The Controlling cycle works like this:

- WOOD breaks up EARTH (think of a new crop pushing up through the soil, or of tree roots pushing down into the earth)

- EARTH dams or muddies WATER

- WATER puts out FIRE

- FIRE melts METAL

- METAL chops WOOD

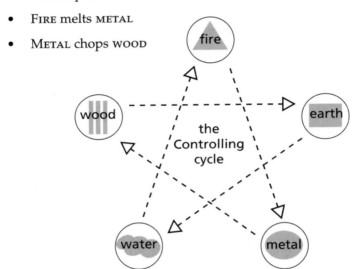

Make sure the controlling element is strong and supported. If you try to put out a bonfire with a tea-cup full of water, the water will evaporate without having much effect. Keep in mind that:

- Too much WOOD can take the edge off METAL

- Too much METAL can overwhelm FIRE

- Too much FIRE evaporates WATER

- Too much WATER can wash EARTH away

- Too much EARTH can smother WOOD

Putting it all Together

The key to working with the elements is to focus on which effect you want to have in a specific space or situation:

- If you want to increase the strength of an element, add the two elements that come before it in the Creative cycle.

- If you want to decrease the strength of an element, use the Controlling cycle *or* the two elements that follow it in the Creative cycle.

Let's say you want to strengthen WOOD energy in a space to support wealth and new beginnings. One way to do this is to add more WOOD energy in the form of plants, flowers, tall shapes, and/or the color green.

If you want to be more sophisticated, you can also add WATER, which feeds WOOD (the Creative Cycle). The expert touch is to remember that feeding WOOD is going to reduce the strength of WATER somewhat, so you can support it by adding a little bit of the METAL element.

"But," you ask, "doesn't METAL chop down WOOD? So isn't that counterproductive?"

Glad you were paying attention! Not to worry, though. First of all, you're going to add a touch of METAL, not a lot. Second, if you give METAL a choice of creating WATER or chopping WOOD, it will prefer to create WATER. Now you've linked three elements in a Creative sequence:

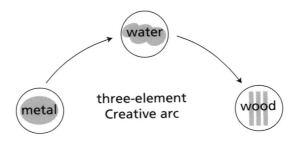

three-element
Creative arc

Using three elements in this way is more powerful than just using one or two. Get in the habit of thinking in threes when you work with the elements, and your feng shui cures will be much more effective.

Let's say that you feel stressed and hyper and have trouble relaxing when you get home from work. Looking around with feng shui eyes, you notice that your den—where you've been trying to unwind—has lots of FIRE energy. The walls and furnishing are red and the focal point of the room is a large fireplace. In addition, you've filled the room with house plants, so now all that WOOD energy is feeding the FIRE.

Taming the FIRE energy in this room will help you relax. One way to do that is with the Controlling cycle, so you might think to put a soothing water fountain in the room. Because the FIRE energy is so strong, however, that one fountain will not have much effect. Plus, with all those plants around, the WATER you've just added is feeding the WOOD, which in turn is feeding the FIRE. You've just created the opposite effect of what you intended!

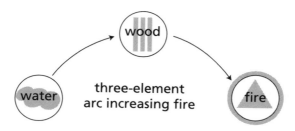

A better way is to use the Creative cycle. By adding EARTH and METAL energy, you not only bring in the elements that will help ground and focus you, but you also direct the FIRE energy into a creative outlet. You might paint the walls a soothing beige, place an ornamental brass box or platter on the coffee table, and curl up in a brown chenille blanket as you relax on the couch.

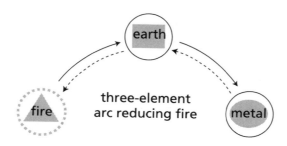

28

The Elements and the Ba Gua

Each *gua* is associated with one of the elements, as shown below. There are three earth *guas* (including the *tai chi*), two wood and metal *guas*, and one *gua* each for water and fire.

Pale green—the color of new growth in the spring —is associated with *jen gua* (family); darker greens—the color of mature plants and trees—are associated with *hsun gua* (wealth). *Hsun gua* is also associated with the color purple, because that color is symbolic of wealth.

Kun gua, the relationship area, is associated with the nurturing, feminine qualities of EARTH. While any of the EARTH colors would be appropriate in that area, *kun gua* is specifically associated with the colors red, pink, and white, because it is located between *li gua* (fame; red) and *dui gua* (creativity; white), and because pink is the color of romance. *Chien gua*, (helpful friends) which is METAL, is also associated with the color grey, because it is located between the pure white color of METAL *dui gua* and the black color of *kan gua* (career; WATER).

hsun	*li*	*kun*
wealth	fame	relationships
WOOD	FIRE	EARTH
green & purple	red	pink
jen	*tai chi*	*dui*
family	health	creativity
WOOD	EARTH	METAL
green	yellow	white
ken	*kan*	*chien*
self-understanding	career	helpful friends
EARTH	WATER	METAL
brown	black	white & grey

Each element is naturally strong in some *guas* and weak in others, information that you can use to fine-tune your feng shui adjustments. See the Five Elements Reference Chart on the next page for details.

FIVE ELEMENT REFERENCE CHART

Element	Qualities	Colors	Shapes	Strong in	Weak in	Creates	Reduces	Controls	Controlled by
WOOD	uplifting growing initiating	greens light blues	tall narrow upright	jen hsun kan	dui chien li	fire	water	earth	metal
FIRE	active radiating empowering	reds purples hot orange	triangles pointed sharp	li jen hsun	kan ken kun	earth	wood	metal	water
EARTH	settling grounding stabilizing	browns yellows beiges	square rectangles flat hollow	ken kun tai chi li	jen hsun dui chien	metal	fire	water	wood
METAL	focused internalizing analyzing	white gold & silver metallics	round oval curved arcs	dui chien ken kun	li kan	water	earth	wood	fire
WATER	flowing connecting communicating	black dark blue	wavy irregular sinuous	kan dui chien	ken kun jen hsun	wood	metal	fire	earth

The Power of Your Intention

On an energetic level, you are intricately connected to everything in your home. This means that the strength of your intention to change your life is an integral part of the success of your feng shui cures. If you make generic feng shui adjustments that are not targeted to your own issues and goals, you will not have a strong emotional involvement in what you are doing. Without emotional involvement, it is difficult to trigger significant changes in your life.

Your thoughts are remarkably powerful. Think of the difference in your own energy when you are excited about something, compared to times when you feel lonely, unhappy, or depressed. As you feng shui your home, support your actions with an attitude of enthusiasm and anticipation. When you constantly dwell on how dissatisfied you are with a life situation, your energy becomes stuck there. Apply feng shui with confidence, optimism, and a sense of adventure. This will keep you motivated and help activate the energy of your home.

The empowerment process explained below greatly enhances your efforts by focusing the power of your mind on what you are doing. When you focus your mind on your reasons for making a feng shui adjustment and what you hope to achieve as a result, your feng shui will be much more effective. Activating feng shui with the power of your mind is a crucial element to your success.

Using Intention to Empower Your Changes

One of the key ingredients to success with feng shui is to use the combined power of your body, speech, and mind to activate and reinforce the changes you are making to your home.

The traditional Black Sect method of empowerment is to make your changes, then use the "dispelling mudra" nine times while repeating the mantra, *om mani padme hum,* nine times. (To make the dispelling *mudra,* point your index and pinky fingers straight out while curling your middle and ring finger toward the palm and holding them in place with your thumb. Women, use your right hand; men use your left hand. Now flick the middle and ring finger out, dispelling negative energy.) In this method, the *mudra,* or hand gesture represents the power of body; the *mantra* is the power of speech, and visualizing your desired outcome while you use the *mantra* and *mudra* is the power of mind.

Many clients have said they feel silly chanting in Sanskrit while flicking their fingers in the air. In response to their requests for a more comfortable method, I developed the following variation:

1. **Focus on your intention**: Practice mindful awareness while you are making feng shui changes, so that your physical actions have power and intent behind them. This is the "body" reinforcement.

2. **Make an affirmation**: After you have made your adjustment, make a statement that clearly defines the intended shift in your energy or circumstances. You can say this out loud, whisper it softly to yourself, or even express it subvocally. This is the "speech" reinforcement.

3. **Visualize your desired outcome**: Following your affirmation, take a moment to visualize your desired outcome in your mind, as if it has already taken place. Make your visualization as specific and concrete as possible, using all of your senses, so that you experience the feeling of joy, satisfaction, or relief that your desired results will bring. This is the "mind" reinforcement.

Specific suggestions for using this method are included in the Quick Tips for Principles 2-7. You can follow the suggestions as they are presented, or come up with your own versions. If you feel inspired to close the empowerment with "Let it be done," or "May the blessings be," or a similar phrase, you may certainly do so.

You can repeat the affirmation and visualization steps daily for three, nine, or 27 days for even stronger effect. This is an excellent way to maintain your focus over time, and to help shift both your own energy and the energy of your home. If you decide to do this, it's okay to vary the affirmations and visualizations that you use—you're sure to think of new details as you go along.

AFFIRMATIONS

Affirmations should be phrased in the present tense. Saying something "will" happen implies that it will take place in the future—which means you will never experience it in the present. Use "now" or whatever phrase will put your affirmation in the present tense. Instead of saying, "I *will* open myself to experience all that life has to offer," say, "I *now* open myself to experience all that life has to offer."

VISUALIZATION

Visualization involves both seeing a desired change in your mind's eye and feeling the joy and satisfaction of having achieved your desires. You know you are *feeling* the desired change if there's a smile on your face and your heart feels light and expansive. If you're not smiling, and your body feels tight and heavy, you are still feeling lack and want. It is important to achieve this emotional shift to a feeling of joy and celebration. Don't be discouraged if it's not easy to feel the emotional shift at first. It will come with practice.

TIMING

Between 11AM–1PM, and 11PM–1AM, the energy of the day is shifting; these are good times to empower feng shui changes. If these hours are inconvenient, find a time when you will be calm, alert, and not distracted or interrupted.

Two excellent books about using the power of your mind and emotions to create change are Shakti Gawain's classic, Creative Visualization, *and* Excuse Me, Your Life is Waiting, *by Lynn Grabhorn. See the Resources pages in the back of this book for more information.*

Working with Your
Feng Shui Type

Ideally you will read through this entire book to learn more about feng shui and to find all the Quick Tips that will help you uncover feng shui problems and move toward your goals. Since many of you are likely to be in a hurry, however, I've put together some guidelines to help you focus on the kinds of feng shui changes that are most likely to be an issue for you.

Remember the five element quiz you did on page 21? If you skipped it, take a moment now to go back and find out what your feng shui style is. Then, read about your style below or on the following pages to find out where you most need to focus your feng shui efforts. If you still aren't sure of your feng shui style, read through the paragraphs below and see which one sounds most like you and your home.

NEAT FREAK

Your home is so neat and tidy that it may be a little rigid, sterile, or monochromatic. You tend to like the minimalist look, and are the most likely type to have all-white decor. Bring some natural energy and color into your space in the form of living plants and flowers, and don't shy away from adding personal touches here and there. If all your artwork is abstract, find a place to display a few favorite photographs of friends and family members, so there are some human images around you. Your love for clean, simple spaces and attention to detail mean you are probably on top of any maintenance or clutter issues, so focus on creating a good flow of *chi* through your home (Principle 3), neutralizing any negative influences (Principle 6) and activating your power spots (Principle 7). Your clean and tranquil home is a wonderful environment for the self-nurturing methods described in Principle 8.

PACKRAT

Your biggest problem is clutter! Closets are overflowing, books are stacked two deep on every shelf, you've saved every greeting card you ever got, and all the flat surfaces in your home are piled with stuff. You might still be able to breathe, but your space isn't getting any *chi* at all. Create some breathing room in your house before you do anything else (Principle 5), or you'll just activate all your clutter. Chances are you've been feeling stuck, so focus on getting rid of the old to make room for the new before you do anything else. Once you've cleared out enough stuff to get a good look at your house, make sure you've got a good flow of *chi* through the space (Principle 3) and address any maintenance issues (Principle 4) before tackling Principles 6 and 7. Your own *chi* will shift a lot as you clean out your home, so be sure to practice some of the grounding and balancing methods in Principle 8.

FREE SPIRIT

You've been feng shui-ing your home since the day you moved in, even if you didn't know what to call it. You are the type most likely to want to work on everything, so be sure to define some priorities (Principle 1) before jumping into changes. Your enthusiasm for creative décor may lead you to overlook basic maintenance issues and allow clutter to pile up. Take care of those first (Principles 3-5), then make sure that you are applying your individuality to your power spots rather than scattering it randomly about the place (Principle 2). Make sure that you haven't overlooked any hidden feng shui problems (Principle 6), and use your creativity to develop your own unique feng shui enhancements (Principle 7). You've probably tried some of the personal renewal methods described in Principle 8 over the years, but may not have kept up a consistent practice. Make a commitment to pay as much attention to the inner you as you do to your surroundings.

GO-GETTER

Your house is probably beautifully furnished and well maintained, but you may have delegated so many of your home-maintenance chores that you no longer have a strong energetic attachment to your space.

Make sure you don't delegate all your feng shui tasks, too, or they won't have much power behind them. Find small, simple things you can do yourself and be sure to put some of your own energy into enhancing your power spots (Principle 7). If you arrange for someone else to take care of other feng shui chores (Principles 3-6), it will be especially important to perform the body-speech-mind empowerments on each one when the work is done. Chances are good you've been pushing yourself pretty hard for a long time, so be sure to pick a few ways to balance and renew your own *chi* from Principle 8.

WHIRLWIND

You're usually moving too fast to pay much attention to your house, but once you get into feng shui you'll want to do it all in one afternoon. Do some planning before you begin, or you'll jump from one unnecessary enhancement to another without getting to the important stuff. You want to start with Principle 7 because it looks like the most fun, but if you skip Principles 1 and 2 you won't know where to begin, and overlooking Principles 3-6 could sabotage your other efforts. Instead of reading this book at home—where you're liable to jump up to make the first change you read about—why not take it on your next business trip? If you read it on the plane with a pad of sticky notes you'll return home with important pages flagged and a list of key changes to make. You'll benefit from the discipline of empowering your changes with a daily ritual—it's an essential part of the process, and the thing you're most likely to skip! Pamper yourself with something from Principle 8, and you'll be amazed how much calmer you feel.

the
$\mathscr{F}$AST FENG SHUI
Principles

Principle 1

Know What You Want

Having a clear goal in mind for what you want to change about your life enables you to identify the areas of the *ba gua*—and the corresponding areas of your home—on which you will concentrate your feng shui efforts.

It's a good idea to focus your feng shui activity on one main issue at a time, so the energy shifts that you trigger will be targeted to that aspect of your life. If you've been living in the same home with the same belongings in the same place for years, making a lot of changes at once will really stir things up, and the results can be chaotic. If you try to do too much at once, you may become overwhelmed with choices, get bogged down in lots of little details, and lose your momentum. You may even start feeling that things are too much of a mess to fix, and become discouraged.

Even if you feel you want to change everything in your life and are really ready to bust out of your rut, it's a good idea to proceed with just a few changes at first. If a particular change makes you uncomfortable, it's helpful to be able to pinpoint what you did to trigger it, so you can put it things back the way they were until you're ready to move forward again.

Quick Tips 1-3 help you to define specific goals for
what you would like to achieve through feng shui.

Issues Assessment

Some people come to feng shui with a specific problem or issue they want to address. Others have so many things they want to change that they try to do too much at once. Somewhere in the middle are those who are drawn to feng shui for reasons they may not be able to articulate. They know it is something they want to explore, but without a specific problem to be resolved they don't know where to start.

Listed on the next page are some of the life issues that may manifest when there is a problem with a specific area of the *ba gua*. Even when these issues are not specifically caused by poor feng shui, they can be addressed by improving the *chi* of that *gua*.

Use this Issues Assessment to help you define what areas of your life you want to work on. (It's a good idea to photocopy the assessment page, or to write your answers on a separate sheet of paper, so you can do the assessment again at a later date.)

First, rate each statement based on how accurately it reflects how you feel about your life at this time. Use the following scale:

5 = Not true for me at all; I'm happy with the way things are

4 = Not very true, but there is some room for improvement

3 = Some relevance to me, but it's not a major issue right now

2 = Mostly true, although things could be worse

1 = This is definitely a problem area for me

Then, total up the ratings for each *gua*. The *gua* with the lowest rating is your priority area for change. If you have two or more low contenders, pick one to start with. Remember that you want to focus your feng shui efforts, not dilute them by trying to change too many things at once.

Use a separate sheet of paper for your answers, or photocopy this page, so you can repeat the Assessment in a few months.

RATING
issue   gua

KAN
(*career*)
I have no idea what I should do with my life ....

I am feeling dissatisfied with my career ....

I find it hard to meet people or make friends ....

KEN
(*self-understanding*)
My life seems empty or lacks spirituality ....

I would like to be in or getting more from therapy ..

I feel stressed and ungrounded most of the time ......

JEN
(*family*)
I have a difficult relationship with my family ....

My health is poor *or* I wish I had more vitality ....

It is hard for me to get going on new projects ....

HSUN
(*wealth*)
I'm having a hard time financially ....

I'm making good money, but can't seem to save ......

Nothing is enough for me, I always want more ....

LI
(*fame*)
I am having legal problems ....

My reputation is holding me back ....

I am not getting the recognition that I deserve ....

KUN
(*relationships*)
My love life is non-existent or unfulfilling ....

I have unresolved issues with my mother ....

I take better care of others than I do of myself ....

DUI
(*creativity*)
I am feeling blocked and frustrated creatively ....

I worry about my kids *or* I want to have a baby ....

I find it hard to complete the projects I start ....

CHIEN
(*helpful friends*)
I want to travel *or* I am tired of constant traveling ...

I feel like there's nobody on my side ....

I have unresolved issues with my father ....

Quick Tip **1** Keep a feng shui journal

Use a notebook or journal to write down your feng shui goals, actions, and results. You can use your notebook to:

- Make a list of all the specific changes you would like to experience as a result of feng shui

- Sketch your floor plan, and annotate it with problem areas to deal with and/or changes you plan to make

- Make notes on what you plan to do as you choose priorities and decide on tasks

- Make shopping lists for the hardware/housewares store

- Write down the affirmations and visualizations you will use to empower your feng shui changes (Tip 2)

- Record specific changes you make to your home, including when and why you made them

- Explore any emotional issues that come up for you as a result of your feng shui changes

Your notebook doesn't have to be fancy, but it should be new so it has clean energy. It should be small enough so it is easy to carry around, yet large enough to write and sketch in easily. Good sizes are 5"x7" or 6"x9".

Be prepared to really use your notebook: stuff things in it, tear pages out, be creative. As soon as you start changing things around in your home, your own energy will start to shift as well. When you do feng shui, you are likely to find yourself more creative in all aspects of life, seeing things from new angles and having new ideas. Write them all down!

Quick Tip 2 Be able to see and feel your success

You know by now that your strong, focused intention is a very powerful item in your feng shui tool box. Now that you have identified your primary desires for change, you can define a goal and create a clear, specific mental image of what achieving that goal will mean to you.

Get out your feng shui notebook, and take a few minutes to think about your answers to the following questions.

- What is my most important goal for feng shui at this time?

- How do I want that to manifest? (be specific!)

- How will my environment change as a result?

- What new possessions do I hope to acquire?

- What new experiences will I have?

- What different activities will I participate in?

- Who will I spend more (or less) time with?

- What new or favorite places will I spend time in?

- What different feelings do I expect or want to have?

For example, if you hope to increase your prosperity with feng shui, think about what you will do with that new abundance. You want to be able to see yourself completing all of the steps that lead to your goal.

Here are some of the things you might visualize if your goal is increased prosperity and abundance:

- Making deposits to your checking and investment accounts

- Opening account statements and seeing your higher balances

- Sitting at your desk writing and signing checks to pay bills, knowing that there is plenty of money available to take care of all of them, with an ample amount left over

- Writing "paid in full" on your receipts
- Putting the checks into envelopes
- Sealing and stamping the envelopes
- Dropping the paid bills in the mail
- Receiving your next credit card statement and seeing a "$0" balance
- Looking in your wallet and seeing it full of $100 bills
- Paying cash for an item you currently can't afford
- Driving around town in your new car
- Purchasing that new couch you've wanted
- Strolling along the beach with your sweetheart on a luxury vacation

...and so on. Be sure to include specific outcomes that reflect what you really want to experience.

Remember to include the three-step empowerment process as part of your feng shui actions:

1. Focus on your **intention** while you are making the change
2. Reinforce your intention with a specific **affirmation**, once the change has been made
3. **Visualize** the desired change, as if it has already happened, with a feeling of joy and satisfaction

Remember that affirmations should always be phrased in the present tense, and that your visualization should produce a feeling of happiness and contentment.

Quick Tip **3**   Make a feng shui collage

A collage of images that represent things you would like to have or experience in your life is a powerful feng shui tool, and a fun way to explore your objectives.

For a large collage, use a piece of poster board (available at any art supply store); 20" x 30" is a good size. A letter-size manila folder makes a good portable collage. Open, it will stand up on a desk or shelf. Folded, you can slip it into your briefcase or tote bag and sneak a peak from time to time during the day. Refer to the five elements chart on page 30, then chose a color of folder or poster board that matches the type of energy you most feel in need of right now. Red is always a good choice because it symbolizes wealth and success.

You will also need scissors, a glue stick, and lots of magazines. A collage is especially powerful if there's an image of you in it, so dig out a couple of snapshots of yourself and photocopy them in several sizes, so you'll have a selection to choose from.

Go through the magazines and tear out pages that have images or phrases that appeal to you. Work intuitively, and include whatever appeals to you in the moment.

Cut out lots of words and pictures, then go through them all and select your favorites. Lay a few main images out on your board before gluing them down, and play with the layout. It's a good idea to do your cutting first, and then paste up words and images as a separate step. If you paste as you go along, you're liable to run out of room for even better images you come across deeper in your magazine pile.

Don't expect to use everything you cut out. If you enjoy the collage process, save your leftover words and images to use next time. You may want to start an ongoing file to which you can add collage-worthy items whenever you come across them.

When your collage is done, explore the images you've included and the associations that they have for you. For example, perhaps you cut out a picture of someone riding a horse along a beach, and pasted your own face on top of the rider's. What does this image mean to you? For one person it might trigger the realization that a great vacation is long overdue. For another, it could mean finding the courage to try new things. Someone else might associate the same picture with gaining much-desired personal freedom.

Place your collage in one of your power spots (you'll learn where these are in Principle 2), where you will see it frequently.

THROW A COLLAGE PARTY
Get together with a few good friends and have a collage party. You'll get a better selection of magazines this way, and it's fun at the end of the session to each show off your creations and explain what the symbolism means to you.

INTENTION—As you make your collage, focus on creating positive changes in your life.

AFFIRMATION—When you are done, make a statement to support your intention, such as: "I now achieve everything I desire in life, including [your specific goals]," or "All the wonderful things represented in this collage now manifest for me with perfect timing and in perfect ways."

VISUALIZATION—Take a few moments to admire what you have created, and visualize all the wonderful changes coming into your life as though they have already happened.

Principle 2

꙳

Locate Your Power Spots

In most homes, there will be many details of the layout, furniture placement, and home decor that could be improved through feng shui. If you try to make every possible feng shui adjustment, you risk diluting your efforts by putting time and effort into correcting minor things.

POWER SPOTS are the areas of your home that are most directly related to your key issues. When you know where your power spots are, you know where to focus your energy and activity. Instead of trying to fix every detail, begin by working on those areas that will have the greatest impact on your key needs for progress. Keep in mind that even a small change can have a big effect if it is in the right place.

Identifying your personal power spots depends on what your key objectives are at this time. For example, let's say that you and your neighbor live in identical homes but that you want to address relationship issues and she wants to improve her career. Your power spots will be your bedroom and the relationship *guas* of your house; hers will be her home office and the career *guas* of her house.

Expect your power spots to change over time. As you address the issues that are most important to you now, you will move on to focus on other areas of your life. Six months or a year from now your power spots should be different from where they are today, because feng shui is all about creating change in your life.

Now that you've identified your priority issue (Principle 1), let's find the power spots where you will focus your feng shui efforts. It is extremely helpful to use a floor plan of your home at this stage (keep a clean original, and make about a half-dozen photocopies).

47

First, find the room or rooms that are associated with the aspect of your life you would like to work on. We're not using the *ba gua* yet; at this stage we are simply identifying what places in your home are used for the activities most closely associated with your key issue, or that have symbolic association with those issues. Typically these are:

- CAREER—front door (associated with opportunities); home office, if you have one; any space where you work at home, or that you study in if you are taking classes related to your career

- MONEY—home office, if you have one; kitchen (associated with your ability to earn a good income); wherever you usually take care of your finances and pay the bills

- RELATIONSHIPS—your bedroom; your living room; anyplace where you and your partner usually spend time together

- FAMILY—living room or den; dining room

- HEALTH—bedroom; kitchen; dining room

- CREATIVITY—home office or studio

Mark these areas on your floor plan. In some cases, such as if you have a home office in a corner of your bedroom or living room, the area associated with your key issue may be only part of a room.

Now look for the areas on the *ba gua* that correspond to your key issue. (You may want to refer to the *ba gua* map on page 16.) Look at:

1. The *ba gua* of your entire property, if you have a yard.

2. The *ba gua* of your entire house or apartment. (If your house has more than one storey, remember to orient the *ba gua* for each level to where you enter it—usually this is at the top or bottom of a stairway.)

3. The *ba gua* of each key room you identified above.

Use a separate copy of your floor plan for each of these *ba guas* (property, house, individual rooms), for easier reference. Mark key *guas* on each floor plan, and compare them to the key rooms you located.

Look for Areas of Special Strength

Look for rooms related to your key issue that are also l
identified with that issue—the relevant *gua* within that room is going
to be a very strong power spot for feng shui improvements.

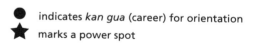

●   indicates *kan gua* (career) for orientation

★   marks a power spot

a relationship power spot: *kun gua* of the bedroom
is also in *kun gua* of the house

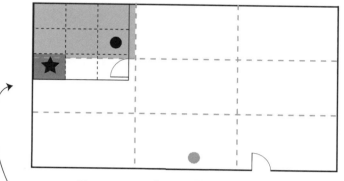

a wealth power spot: home office is mostly in *hsun gua*
of the house; *hsun gua* within the the office is a good
position for the desk

Look for EXTENSIONS that add to the strength of your priority *guas*. An extension is a place where a part of the home sticks out of the floor plan. The part that sticks out must be less than one-half the total length or width of that side of the house to be considered an extension.

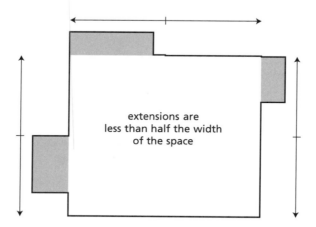

extensions are
less than half the width
of the space

An extension in a *gua* means that the energy of that *gua* is very strong. If your house has an extension in any of your priority *guas*, the feng shui enhancements you place there will be very powerful.

Sometimes you will find an extension when you look at the *ba gua* of a particular room. This type of extension strengthens the *gua* within that room, but does not affect the entire house.

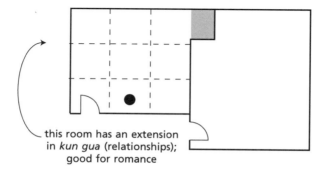

this room has an extension
in *kun gua* (relationships);
good for romance

50

Look for Areas of Weakness

Look for missing areas that are detracting from the strength of your priority *guas*. A missing area is a place where there is a "bite" out of the floor plan. The gap must be less than one-half the total length or width of that side of the house to be considered missing.

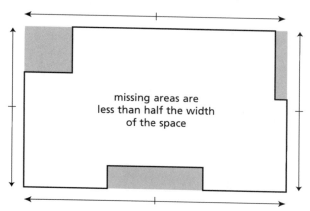

missing areas are
less than half the width
of the space

A missing area in a *gua* means that the energy of that *gua* is weak. If there is a missing area in any of your priority rooms or *guas* you will want to use feng shui to strengthen that area.

Sometimes you will find a missing area when you look at the *ba gua* of a particular room. This missing area will weaken the affected gua in that room, but does not affect the rest of the house.

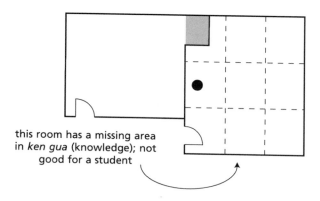

this room has a missing area
in *ken gua* (knowledge); not
good for a student

51

Many homes and apartments are very irregular in shape, and it can be difficult to determine whether or not a possible missing area is a problem. Use your own experience to guide you.

First, look at what *gua* is affected, in terms of the shape of the home. Think about the implications of a weakness in that *gua*; are you having major problems in the related areas of your life? Has there been a significant shift in that aspect of your life since you moved into that home?

If so, look for ways to strengthen that *gua*, either by correcting the missing area or by strengthening secondary guas in major rooms of the house (see Tip 4).

If you are not having major problems with those life-aspects, look for more important changes to work on first. Remember, feng shui is just one factor affecting your life, and your own personal *chi* (or luck, or whatever) may be strong enough to overcome that issue on its own.

Direct Your Focus

Use the results of this process to direct where you will focus your feng shui efforts. For example, if you have a clutter problem, ideally you want to get rid of all of your clutter, in every part of your house. Fast Feng Shui makes the process manageable by directing you to clean up the clutter problem in your power spots first, before working on the rest of your space.

Try to have no more than three major power spots. If you come up with more than that, divide them into "A" and "B" priorities.

Quick Tip 4 tells you how to correct a "missing" *gua*.
Tips 5-15 suggest specific places you may want to focus your efforts, based on your key issue.

Quick Tip 4 How to correct a missing gua

EXTERIOR CURES

You can correct a missing area by placing a light, flag pole, bird bath, large stone, statue, or tree in the exact spot where the corner of the building would be if the area were not missing. You can also use a floral border, hedge, or fence to define where the walls would be if the area

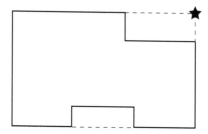

were not missing. Your placement must be very accurate for the cure to be effective. A few inches out of alignment will make a difference!

If you already have a porch, deck, balcony, or patio that takes up that space, here are some ways to activate it:

- Place a light or plant at the outside corner

- Place a row of plants along the railing

- Wrap a strand of lights or flags around the railing

- Plant a hedge to border the patio

If your home is a very irregular shape, focus on creating a more complete shape rather than curing every irregularity, then strengthen important *guas* inside the home.

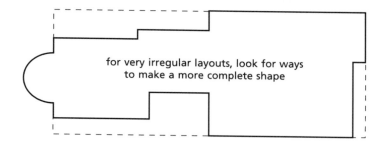

for very irregular layouts, look for ways to make a more complete shape

INTERIOR CURES

You can correct a missing area by placing a large mirror on an interior wall so that the reflection implies a virtual room where there is none. For even better effect, place something with symbolic imagery related to your goals where the mirror will reflect it into the space.

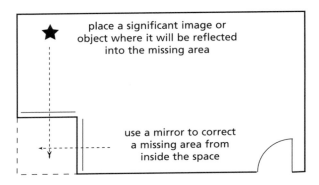

place a significant image or object where it will be reflected into the missing area

use a mirror to correct a missing area from inside the space

INTENTION—As you install your cures, focus on completing or correcting the missing *gua(s)* energetically.

AFFIRMATION—When you are done, make a statement to support your intention, such as: "My Relationship *gua* is now whole and strong, strengthening and completing my love life in all ways," or "My Fortunate Blessings *gua* is now complete, bringing greater prosperity and abundance into my life."

VISUALIZATION—Take a moment to imagine that any real or potential weakness in the corresponding area of your life has been remedied. Visualize a specific enhancement you would like to experience in your life as a result of correcting this missing *gua*, and imagine that it has already happened for you.

STRENGTHEN SECONDARY GUAS

If using a mirror is not appropriate, or you don't like the way it looks, you can bring your home into better balance by strengthening other *guas* inside the home.

For example, if a relationship *gua* is missing or weak, strengthen the relationship areas of the bedroom and living room. If the wealth *gua* is missing, strengthen the wealth areas in the bedroom, living room, and kitchen. If your career *gua* is missing, make a big deal out of the main entrance and foyer, and make sure the career *guas* in your living room and home office are strong. (You'll learn about specific ways to enhance each *gua* in Principle 7.)

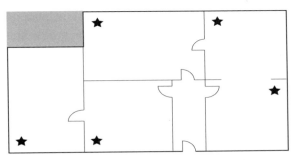

this house has a missing corner in *hsun gua* (wealth);
correct by strengthening *hsun gua* of major rooms

INTENTION—As you enhance secondary *guas*, focus on balancing the energy of your home.

AFFIRMATION—When you are done, make a statement to support your intention, such as: "*Dui gua* is now corrected, enhancing my creativity and helping me to complete projects on time."

VISUALIZATION—Take a moment to visualize the *chi* of that *gua* being full and strong. Imagine that a specific improvement you have in mind has already happened.

Quick Tip **5** If your key issue is Career...

BEGIN BY WORKING ON:

- *Kan gua* (career)
- Front door and path (communication and opportunities)
- *Li gua* (reputation)

THEN PAY ATTENTION TO:

- *Chien gua* (helpful friends)
- *Ken gua* (self-understanding)
- *Dui gua* (creativity)

QUICK TIPS FOR YOUR CAREER

The Quick Tips shown below are often helpful for people with career issues. Other tips may also apply, depending on your situation and the unique qualities and challenges of your space.

PRINCIPLE	TIPS
3. Create a Path for Chi	17, 20, 21, 22 and 28
4. Repaint, Repair, Renew	36, 37 and 38
5. Clean Up Your Clutter	46, 52 and 58
6. Neutralize Negative Influences	63, 64, 72 and 75
7. Activate Your Power Spots	83 and 87
8. Work on Yourself...	98 and 105

Quick Tip **6** If your key issue is Self-Understanding...

BEGIN BY WORKING ON:

- *Ken gua* (self-understanding)
- Your personal *chi* (Principle 8)
- EARTH energy

THEN PAY ATTENTION TO:

- Creating a space for quiet self-reflection
- Condition and placement of mirrors (self-perception)
- Condition of windows (ability to see things clearly)

QUICK TIPS FOR SELF-UNDERSTANDING AND SPIRITUALITY

The Quick Tips shown below are often helpful for people with self-understanding and/or spirituality issues. Other tips may also apply, depending on your situation and the unique qualities and challenges of your space.

PRINCIPLE	TIPS
3. Create a Path for Chi	22 and 28
4. Repaint, Repair, Renew	38, 40 and 43
5. Clean Up Your Clutter	49, 55 and 56
6. Neutralize Negative Influences	59
7. Activate Your Power Spots	79 and 88
8. Work on Yourself...	102, 103, 104 and 105

Quick Tip 7 If your key issue is Family...

BEGIN BY WORKING ON:

- *Jen gua* (family)
- Living and dining rooms (family gathering places)

THEN PAY ATTENTION TO:

Guas associated with family members:

hsun oldest daughter	*li* middle daughter	*kun* mother
jen oldest son	*tai chi* 	*dui* youngest daughter
ken youngest son	*kan* middle son	*chien* father

QUICK TIPS FOR FAMILY RELATIONSHIPS

The Quick Tips shown below are often helpful for people with family issues. Other tips may also apply, depending on your situation and the unique qualities and challenges of your space.

PRINCIPLE	TIPS
3. Create a Path for Chi	16, 19, 23 and 24
4. Repaint, Repair, Renew	32, 34, 43 and 44
5. Clean Up Your Clutter	48 and 49
6. Neutralize Negative Influences	59, 61, 62, 63, 65 and 77
7. Activate Your Power Spots	89
8. Work on Yourself...	97 and 105

Quick 8 Tip If your key issue is Prosperity...

BEGIN BY WORKING ON:

- *Hsun gua* (wealth)
- Kitchen stove (prosperity)
- Plumbing maintenance

THEN PAY ATTENTION TO:

- WATER energy
- *Li gua* (fame)
- *Chien gua* (helpful friends)

QUICK TIPS FOR MONEY AND PROSPERITY

The Quick Tips shown below are often helpful for people with money issues. Other tips may also apply, depending on your situation and the unique qualities and challenges of your space.

PRINCIPLE	TIPS
3. Create a Path for Chi	17, 20, 22, 23, 24 and 28
4. Repaint, Repair, Renew	35, 36, 39, 41 and 42
5. Clean Up Your Clutter	46, 48, 51, 52 and 58
6. Neutralize Negative Influences	59, 60 and 72
7. Activate Your Power Spots	81, 83, 90 and 96
8. Work on Yourself...	105

Quick **9**
Tip **9** If your key issue is Fame...

BEGIN BY WORKING ON:
- *Li gua* (fame and reputation)
- FIRE energy
- Lighting and mirrors

THEN PAY ATTENTION TO:
- First impressions (exterior maintenance, entryway, etc.)
- Neutralizing negative influences (Principle 6)
- *Chien gua* (helpful friends)

QUICK TIPS FOR FAME AND REPUTATION
The Quick Tips shown below are often helpful for people with fame and reputation issues. Other tips may also apply, depending on your situation and the unique qualities and challenges of your space.

PRINCIPLE	TIPS
3. Create a Path for Chi	16, 18 and 19
4. Repaint, Repair, Renew	35, 36, 40 and 43
5. Clean Up Your Clutter	46, 49 and 51
6. Neutralize Negative Influences	59, 61, 62, 63 and 75
7. Activate Your Power Spots	81, 82, 84, 91 and 96
8. Work on Yourself...	98 and 105

Quick Tip **10** If your key issue is Relationships...

BEGIN BY WORKING ON:

- *Kun gua* (relationships)
- Your bedroom
- Your bed

THEN PAY ATTENTION TO:

- *Chien gua* (helpful friends)
- *Kan gua* (social contacts)
- *Ken gua* (self-understanding)

QUICK TIPS FOR LOVE AND MARRIAGE

The Quick Tips shown below are often helpful for people dealing with relationship issues. Other tips may also apply, depending on your situation and the unique qualities and challenges of your space.

PRINCIPLE	TIPS
3. Create a Path for Chi	17, 20 and 22
4. Repaint, Repair, Renew	35, 37, 38 and 40
5. Clean Up Your Clutter	46, 53, 55, and 56
6. Neutralize Negative Influences	59, 65, 70, 74 and 78
7. Activate Your Power Spots	79, 86, 92 and 96
8. Work on Yourself...	98 and 105

Quick Tip 11 If your key issue is Creativity or Children...

Dui is associated with both children and creativity—things that you give birth to. If your issue is creativity, give special attention to your work space; if you are trying to have a baby, your own bedroom and personal *chi* will be important as well.

BEGIN BY WORKING ON:
- *Dui gua* (children and creativity)
- Bedrooms
- Work spaces

THEN PAY ATTENTION TO:
- Light and crystal ball cures
- Balancing personal *chi*

QUICK TIPS FOR CREATIVITY AND FERTILITY
The Quick Tips shown below are often helpful for people with creativity and/or fertility issues. Other tips may also apply, depending on your situation and the unique qualities and challenges of your space.

PRINCIPLE	TIPS
3. Create a Path for Chi	20, 22, 23 and 24
4. Repaint, Repair, Renew	37, 40 and 43
5. Clean Up Your Clutter	46, 47 and 53
6. Neutralize Negative Influences	66, 70, 72 and 74
7. Activate Your Power Spots	79, 84, 85, 93 and 96
8. Work on Yorself...	97, 101 and 105

Quick Tip **12** If your key issue is Helpful Friends or Travel...

If your issue is building a support network, also pay attention to communication and your reputation. If your focus is travel, activate *chien gua* to help your trip come together smoothly through all the other people involved.

BEGIN BY WORKING ON:
- *Chien gua* (helpful friends and travel)
- Doorways
- *Li gua* (fame)

THEN PAY ATTENTION TO:
- Getting rid of old, negative *chi*
- Your car and garage

QUICK TIPS FOR SUPPORT AND TRAVEL
The Quick Tips shown below are often helpful for people with travel/support issues. Other tips may also apply, depending on your situation and the unique qualities and challenges of your space.

PRINCIPLE	TIPS
3. Create a Path for Chi	17, 20 and 21
4. Repaint, Repair, Renew	35, 36, 37, 38 and 44
5. Clean Up Your Clutter	49, 57 and 58
6. Neutralize Negative Influences	75, 76, 77 and 78
7. Activate Your Power Spots	81 and 94
8. Work on Yorself...	97 and 105

Quick Tip **13** If your key issue is Health ...

BEGIN BY WORKING ON:

- Your bedroom and kitchen
- Neutralizing negative *(sha) chi* (Principle 6)
- Your personal *chi* (Principle 8)

ALSO PAY ATTENTION TO:

- Condition of plumbing and electrical systems
- Areas related to specific body parts:

hsun	li	kun
legs, hips, gall bladder	eyes, heart	abdomen, stomach
jen	**tai chi**	**dui**
feet, liver	☯	mouth, lungs
ken	**kan**	**chien**
hands, spleen	ears, kidneys, bladder	head, large intestine

QUICK TIPS FOR HEALTH AND VITALITY

The Quick Tips shown below are often helpful for people with health issues. Other tips may also apply, depending on your situation and the unique qualities and challenges of your space.

PRINCIPLE	TIPS
3. Create a Path for Chi	25, 30 and 31
4. Repaint, Repair, Renew	34, 40 and 42
5. Clean Up Your Clutter	45, 54, 55 and 56
6. Neutralize Negative Influences	63, 65, 66, 68 and 71
7. Activate Your Power Spots	86, 95 and 96
8. Work on Yourself...	100-102, 104 and 105

Quick Tip **14** Other key issues

Here are some other common issues, and their related areas:

ISSUE	LOOK FOR PROBLEMS WITH
Arguments	*Sha* (negative) *chi* in any room or spot where arguments tend to happen (see Principle 6)
Legal problems	*Li gua* (reputation) *Kun gua* (relationships)
Poor grades	Desk placement *Ken gua* (knowledge)
Loneliness	*Kan gua* (social contacts) *Ken gua* (self-understanding) *Chien gua* (helpful friends)
Depression	Personal *chi* Clutter *Li gua* and lighting (inspiration/illumination)
Weight gain	Personal *chi* Clutter *Ken gua* (self-understanding)
Frustration	Clutter Doors and entryways *Dui gua* (creativity)
Indecisiveness	Windows Mirrors *Ken gua* (self-understanding) Weak EARTH element
Lack of confidence	Personal *chi* *Ken gua* (self-understanding) Weak WOOD element

Quick Tip **15** If you still don't know where to start...

BEGIN BY WORKING ON:

- *Ken gua* (self-understanding)
- *Kan gua* (life path)
- Windows and mirrors (ability to see clearly)

THEN PAY ATTENTION TO:

- Creating space in the center of your home
- Opening up any other cluttered or blocked areas
- Enhancing new beginnings (*jen gua*)

QUICK TIPS FOR CLARITY AND DIRECTION

The Quick Tips shown below are often helpful for people who lack clarity. Other tips may also apply, depending on your situation and the unique qualities and challenges of your space.

PRINCIPLE	TIPS
3. Create a Path for Chi	17, 21, 25 and 28
4. Repaint, Repair, Renew	34, 37, 40 and 43
5. Clean Up Your Clutter	45, 46, 47 and 49
6. Neutralize Negative Influences	59, 63, 65 and 75
7. Activate Your Power Spots	81, 88 and 95
8. Work on Yourself...	97 and 105

Principle 3

Create a Path for Chi

One of the objectives of feng shui is to create a smooth, gentle, nurturing flow of *chi* through your home. Your front door is called the "mouth of *chi*" because it is the primary way *chi* enters your home. Focus your first feng shui efforts on any potential problems with your front door and the path from the street, sidewalk, or driveway to your front door. Overgrown hedges, hidden front doors and dim lighting are barriers to *chi*. If your mouth of *chi* has poor feng shui, the *chi* of your entire home will suffer.

Even if you always enter your home through the garage or the side or back door, your formal front door is still the symbolic mouth of *chi*. Think of *chi* as an important guest you wish to welcome to your home, and make your formal entry—and the access to it from the street—as inviting as possible. In turn, this will make it easier for you to emerge from the shelter of your home out into the world, and to return again to your sanctuary at the end of the day.

Inside your home, *chi* likes to flow in gentle curves, and will exit through side doors and windows. Long straight corridors will funnel *chi* very quickly toward whatever is at the far end. Active spaces of your home should have a more active flow of *chi*. *Chi* should slow down and linger in the places you like to sit down and relax at the end of the day, or where you need to focus and concentrate on the work at hand.

One of my first feng shui consultations was for a friend who lived in a poorly maintained apartment building. Here are some of the feng shui problems I encountered before I even got inside her apartment:

- There was no tenant directory in the lobby (fortunately, I knew her apartment number)

- All the apartments except hers had numbers on the door (I found it through the process of elimination)

- My friend was using her maiden name, but her ex-husband's name was the only one on the door, even though he no longer lived there

- There was no doorbell or knocker, and when I knocked on the door she didn't hear me for several minutes

- There was so much stuff behind the door that it only opened a little way. I had to turn sideways to get in.

No wonder this woman was having problems! At each step of the way, starting at the entrance to her building, bad feng shui was keeping any fresh new *chi* from finding its way into her home.

DO A WALK-THROUGH OF YOUR HOME

Starting at your mouth of *chi*, walk slowly and mindfully all through your space. Imagine that you are a gentle stream flowing through your home. What gets in your way? Where do you flow smoothly? Are any areas blocked off from you? Are there places where you become turbulent? Why? Where are you diverted into side pools and eddies? Are there any areas where you flow too swiftly, and what do you crash into at the other end? Pay special attention to the flow of *chi* to your power spots. Make sure that *chi* can get there easily, and that it is neither too turbulent nor too strong when it arrives. If your most important power spot is a long way from the front door, hang a bell or wind chime in the doorway and ring it every time you enter the room, so the sound will attract *chi* to that space

Quick Tips 16-31 show you how to invite fresh, vital *chi* into your home and direct it to your power spots.

Quick Tip **16** Your house number should be easy to see

Do delivery drivers from UPS, your drycleaner, or the local pizza place ever have trouble finding your place? Have guests ever arrived late for dinner, saying, "We drove right past your house." If people can't find your house, *chi* will have a hard time finding it, too.

House numbers and letters are available at most hardware stores, and are easy to put up. If your house number is already clearly posted, when was the last time you looked at it? Do your brass numbers need to be polished? Are all the screws tightly in place? Are self-adhesive numbers still firmly attached? Have painted numbers become chipped or faded from the sun?

If you live in an apartment, make sure your name is listed in the lobby and on the intercom, and that guests can tell which way to go when they get off the elevator on your floor. If your building is not well-posted, ask the superintendent, management committee, or coop board to improve the situation.

INTENTION—As you repair, polish, or install your house numbers, focus on attracting vibrant new *chi* to your address.

AFFIRMATION—Make a statement to support your intention, such as: "New people and opportunities now easily find their way to me."

VISUALIZATION—Take a moment to visualize fresh energy and opportunities filling your home. Focus on the specific outcome you have in mind, and imagine it as if it has already happened.

Quick Tip 17 Your front path should welcome chi

The ideal path to your front door is gently curved, slightly wider at the street end, and wide enough so you can carry a large shopping bag in each hand as you walk up it.

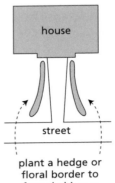

If your path is narrower at the street than at the door, it may be constricting new opportunities from coming your way. One solution is to use plants to create the impression of a wider space at the street end.

plant a hedge or floral border to funnel *chi* up a path that is narrower at the street end

If your path is straight, *chi* may be moving too quickly. Hang a wind chime by your door, and plant some plants or flowers beside the path or at the foot of your front steps to attract your attention and slow *chi* down to a calmer pace.

A flowering apple tree by your front door adds wonderful *chi* to the home, but if you have to duck past a low-hanging branch every day, that's not good feng shui. If bushes and shrubbery have over-grown the sides of the path, it's time to trim them back. Remove anything that turns your path into an obstacle course—greenery, a recycling bin, your kid's tricycle—or your life may feel like an obstacle course as well.

INTENTION—As you clear the path to your door, focus on clearing the way so you can move forward easily in your life. When you have finished, walk up your path and experience how free and confident your progress is now.

AFFIRMATION—Make a statement to support your intention, such as: "I now move smoothly and easily forward in my life."

VISUALIZATION—Visualize opportunities flowing smoothly toward you, while you move confidently out into the world. Make your vision as detailed as you can, as you imagine that your desired results have already been achieved.

Quick Tip 18 Make your front door stand out

Most homes have a clearly defined front door, but some have several entries. If visitors aren't sure which door to knock on, opportunities won't know where to knock, either. More than one main door can also lead to confusion and arguments in the home.

If there are several entries to your home, make sure that one is clearly the most important. Use lighting, plants, or paint to make it clear which is the main entry.

Even if your front door is architecturally prominent, it's a good idea to paint it a contrasting color, so it stands out visually from the color of the surrounding walls. If you live in a semi-detached home, a row of town homes, or in an apartment where there are many identical doors on one hallway, make sure your front door is equal to—or more prominent than—your neighbors.

INTENTION—As you work on making your front door visually prominent, focus on attracting opportunities and *chi* to your home. When you are done, step back so you can admire your front door.

AFFIRMATION—Make a statement to support your intention, such as: "I now welcome bountiful *chi* to my home, in the form of [your specific intention or desire]."

VISUALIZATION—Visualize something specific that you want to attract to your home and life: a new career, a better relationship, a new baby, increased income, etc. Imagine that whatever you desire has already materialized in your life.

Quick Tip 19 Get a new doormat

A doormat marks the transition from public to private and outdoor to indoor space. Is your doormat old, faded, frayed, or full of dirt? Buy a new one, or at least shake it out! Yes, it's better to have that dirt trapped in the doormat than tracked into your house; it's also good feng shui to make the place where people pause before entering your home as well-maintained and attractive as you can.

Semi-circular doormats are friendlier than square ones. If it suits your taste, get one with a sunflower or sun-face design on it. What could be nicer than being greeted by the image of a rising sun every time you open your front door?

Think twice before ordering a custom doormat with your last name woven into it. Do you really want mud all over your family's good name?

If you must have a heavy-duty mud-remover mat, see if you can place it to the side of the door, rather than directly in front of it.

INTENTION—As you put your new doormat in place, focus on making the entrance to your home both functional and attractive.

AFFIRMATION—Make a statement to support your intention, such as: "My home is now a place of peace and tranquility; all worries and stress are left at the door."

VISUALIZATION—Visualize everyone who comes to your home pausing to slow down and shake off stress before entering.

Quick Tip **20** Use your front door

It's amazing how many people rarely use their front door. We have the automobile to thank for this, since it is the reason so many of us now go in and out of our house through the garage most of the time.

When did you last use your front door? Opening it for guests or to sign for a package doesn't count here. Your front door is your home's mouth of *chi*, and if you don't use it you waste all the good *chi* that's piling up there waiting to get in. Not only that, if you come in through the garage all the time, chances are good that you are also entering your house through the utility room or a back hall, both of which are likely to have less than wonderful *chi*.

If you rarely use your front door, make a point of going in and out it from time to time. You'll get a much better flow of good *chi* into the home, and all the effort you put into sprucing up the formal entry to your home won't be wasted.

INTENTION—As you go in and out your front door, focus on activating the "mouth of *chi*" for your home, so more positive energy can nourish your life.

AFFIRMATION—As you use the front door, make a statement to support your intention, such as: "I now welcome vital, nourishing *chi* to fill my home and assist me in [whatever is appropriate to your personal goals]."

VISUALIZATION—Each time you use your front door, take a moment to visualize positive energy flowing into your home and helping you to achieve your goals. Imagine your desired outcome as if it has already happened.

Quick Tip 21 Don't block the entry

Keep the area around your front door clear. The "mouth of *chi*" is too important a space to be obstructed.

This may may not be easy; if you had plenty of space you probably wouldn't be storing stuff there in the first place. Do yourself a favor, and find some other nook or cranny to use if you can. If you absolutely do not have anywhere else but the front entryway to keep stuff, make sure it is stowed as neatly and compactly as possible.

In Hawaii, it's traditional to take off your footwear before entering a home, to avoid tracking dirt inside. This creates the problem of what to do with all those sandals, sneakers, and "slippahs" (rubber flip-flops) that pile up around the door. A large basket solved this problem neatly for us. Unfortunately, I haven't been able to clear the sailboard and other windsurfing equipment out of our front hallway; that really *is* the only place to keep it (and it takes up a *lot* of space).

Do the best you can, and make intelligent compromises if you must. If you can't keep your entryway entirely clear, brighten and energize that space with a higher wattage lightbulb and a faceted crystal ball or wind chime.

INTENTION—As you remove the things you've stored around the front door, focus on welcoming all the blessings and lessons that life has to offer. When you are done, open the door fully, and feel how much more energy is entering in.

AFFIRMATION—Make a statement to support your intention, such as: "I now open myself fully to experiencing all that life has to bring me, including [your specific desire]."

VISUALIZATION—Visualize the new people, opportunities, or situations that you wish to welcome into your life. Imagine that these desires have already manifested for you, and experience a feeling of joy and satisfaction.

Quick
Tip **22** Place a mirror in a small or
narrow entry

What do you see when you enter your front door? If there is a wall less than six feet in front of you, it may be blocking your ability to move forward in your life. The best solution for this is to put a large mirror on that wall:

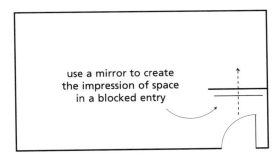

use a mirror to create
the impression of space
in a blocked entry

Make sure the mirror is positioned so you can see yourself fully in it when you enter. If there are others living in your home, be sure to use a mirror that is large enough and hung so that you can each see yourselves when entering. If the mirror is too small, too low, or too high to suit some family members, their self-perception may be affected.

Some feng shui experts feel that a mirror directly opposite the door will bounce the *chi* right back out again. In my opinion this will depend on the specific circumstances of your entryway, and on what is reflected in the mirror. It is just as likely that the mirror will expand and brighten the space, welcoming more *chi* in. Try a mirror, and see how it feels.

If you don't want to place a mirror in your entry, or it just doesn't look right with your décor, another solution is to hang a landscape painting or photograph in the place where a mirror would go. The image should be large and have a distant horizon; this will visually open up the space and allow you to "see" into the distance.

Another problem, the "pinched nose" entry, occurs when the front door opens onto a very narrow hallway. This is thought to restrict the flow of *chi* and opportunities into the home. A pinched nose entry can be corrected by mirroring the wall onto which the door opens:

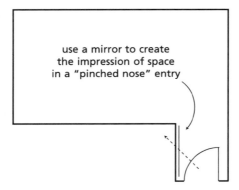

use a mirror to create
the impression of space
in a "pinched nose" entry

INTENTION—As you install a mirror in your entry, focus on removing any constrictions that are affecting that specific *gua* and that may be inhibiting your ability to move forward in your life.

AFFIRMATION—When you are done, make a statement to support your intention, such as: "I now easily and effectively embrace new opportunities and make easy progress on my life's path."

VISUALIZATION—Take a moment to stand in your entryway and experience how much more expansive that area feels with the mirror in place. Visualize new opportunities appearing to you, and see yourself making easy progress toward a specific goal.

Quick Tip 23 Keep chi from flowing out the front door

If you have a stairway leading to the second floor that begins in line with the front door, *chi* could be flowing down the stairs and right out your door. As a general rule, the stairs should end at least one body-length's distance (or about six feet) from the door; ten feet or more is even better.

You can use a basket or potted plant at the foot of the stairs to catch any *chi* that might be flowing down the stairs. Another solution is to hang a faceted crystal ball between the foot of the stairs and the door. You may already have a light fixture in the appropriate spot. Consider replacing it with a small chandelier, or hang a faceted crystal ball below it. If you already have a chandelier in your entry you may not need to do anything more than bless and empower it to prevent *chi* from leaking out the door.

INTENTION—As you place your cure at the foot of the stairs, or hang a faceted crystal ball in your entry, focus on preventing the loss of resources and *chi* from your home.

AFFIRMATION—When you are done, make a statement to support your intention, such as: "Bountiful *chi* is now collected here to nourish my home and family."

VISUALIZATION—Take a moment to visualize *chi* collecting in that area of your home, then flowing to all areas of the house. Think of a specific benefit you would like to achieve by improving the flow of *chi* in your home, and imagine it as if it has already happened.

Quick Tip 24 Keep chi from flowing out the back door

A hallway that cuts straight through your house from the front entry to the back door is thought to funnel *chi* out the back, before it has a chance to nourish the home.

You can slow down the flow of *chi* and direct it to other areas of the house with:

- A carpet or runner with a pattern that runs across the width of the hallway, *and/or*

- A faceted crystal ball, crystal chandelier, or wind chime halfway down the hallway, *or*

- A faceted crystal ball outside the doorway to each room that opens off the corridor, *or*

- A round table in the center of the foyer (if there's enough room) to slow down and redirect *chi*

INTENTION—As you place your cures, focus on preventing *chi* from flowing out the back door before it has had time to nourish your home.

AFFIRMATION—When you are done, make a satement to support your intention, such as: "All areas of my home are now well-nourished by an abundant flow of *chi*."

VISUALIZATION—Stand in your hallway for a few moments and visualize a specific improvement you hope to gain by improving the circulation of *chi* through your home. Picture the desired outcome in your mind as if it has already happened.

Quick Tip 25 Open up your hallways

Hallways are the veins and arteries of your home. If anyone in your family has circulation problems, be sure to remove any clutter from your hallways. Problems with the centerline of the home can also indicate health problems along the centerline of the body. If you have a central hallway, be sure it isn't blocked in any way.

Side tables and bookcases can make a hall feel constricted. If you can't move freely about your house, you may be unable to move freely in your life.

Some homes have a large foyer where *chi* tends to pool before flowing through the rest of the house. If there are multiple rooms opening off this space, *chi* may not know where to go. If the access to any of these rooms is blocked, *chi* will not be able to nourish those spaces. Be thoughtful about how you place furniture, and which doors you leave open (or shut) to help direct *chi* to your power spots.

INTENTION—As you open up your hallways, focus on creating a healthy flow of *chi* through the arteries of your home.

AFFIRMATION—When you are done, make a statement to support your intention, such as: "The hallways of my home are a clear path for *chi* to circulate and nourish every space."

VISUALIZATION—Take a few moments to walk around your home and enjoy your new freedom of movement. Visualize positive energy now circulating easily through your home, and imagine how a specific aspect of your life will benefit from this change.

Quick Tip 26 Use wind chimes to manage chi

The sound waves created by a wind chime will slow down and help disperse *chi* that is moving too quickly. If the path from the street to your front door is long and straight, hang a wind chime by your front door or porch steps to slow the *chi* down so it is a little more gentle as it enters your home.

Wind chimes are also good for lifting the energy of a space. If one corner of your yard is lower than the others, *chi* may settle there. Hanging a wind chime from a tree in that corner can stir the *chi* up and keep it moving.

Wind chimes come in many sizes, from tinkly little tiny ones to great big resonant ones. Match the size of the wind chime to the size of your space. A large brass wind chime might be overwhelming indoors, while a very small chime may not be strong enough to have much effect. Choose metal chimes, as they have a more penetrating tone. The most important consideration for a wind chime is that the sound be pleasing to you, so pick the one whose tones you like the best.

INTENTION—As you hang your wind chime, focus on curing the rushing or sinking *chi* in that spot.

AFFIRMATION—When you are done, make a statement to support your intention, such as: "This beautiful sound now balances and enhances the *chi* of my home"

VISUALIZATION—Take a moment to listen to the chime. Visualize the sound waves balancing and correcting the *chi* of your home. Think of a specific benefit you would like to receive, and imagine that it has already happened for you.

Quick Tip 27 Use faceted crystal balls to redirect chi

Faceted crystal balls are a very popular feng shui cure. In addition to energizing a space, they can interrupt a flow of *chi* that is too strong, and scatter it in many directions, just as they scatter a beam of light into a multitude of rainbow refractions. Good places to hang faceted crystal balls include:

- In the center of a long, narrow hallway
- In front of a window through which too much *chi* is escaping
- Anywhere you'd like to activate *chi*

For added impact, hang your faceted crystal ball from a red string or ribbon, cut to a multiple of nine-inches (9", 18", 27"). The ball can hang any distance from the ceiling; it's the cut length of the string that is important. Tie any extra string into a nice bow or decorative knot. If you buy crystal balls from a feng shui supplier, they may come with red cord already attached. (See the Resources pages at the back of the book for a list of suppliers.)

INTENTION—As you hang your faceted crystal ball, focus on correcting or enhancing the *chi* of that space.

AFFIRMATION—When you are done, make a statement to support your intention, such as: "This crystal catches the *chi* flowing through this room and redirects it to nourish my [aspect of life appropriate to room or *gua*]."

VISUALIZATION—Take a moment to visualize your specific desired outcome as if it has already occurred.

Quick Tip 28   Use the command position

Don't you hate sitting with your back to the door? Just about everyone does, and with good reason; sitting where you can't see the entry makes you feel vulnerable and tense. In addition to not being able to see who's behind you, the *chi* entering that space is hitting you in the back. If your bed, desk, couch, or stove puts you in this position, it will subtly but powerfully increase the level of stress you deal with every day.

In feng shui, we want major pieces of furniture to be positioned so that they give you a view of the doorway, preferably with a solid wall behind you for support, and a little bit off to one side so you are not directly in the path of the *chi* coming in the door:

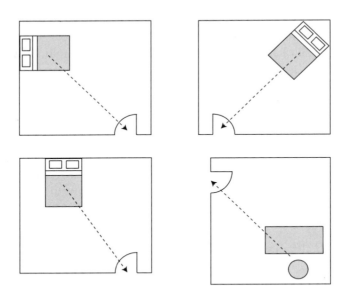

examples of the "command
position"

This is called the "command position," and it will put you more securely in command of your life. As you adjust and direct the flow of *chi* to your power spots, make sure that you arrange your furniture so you will be in the command position.

If you cannot use the command position, hang a mirror so that you will be able to see the door from where you sit or sleep:

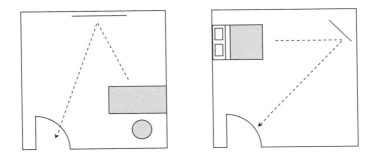

If you cannot use the "command position,"
place a mirror so it gives you a view of the doorway

INTENTION—As you move key furniture into the command position, focus on gaining control over the activities and situations related to that *gua*.

AFFIRMATION—When you are done, make a statement to support your intention, such as: "I am now in a position of strength and power in [appropriate aspect of your life]."

VISUALIZATION—Take a moment to sit in the command position and feel how calm, centered, and in control you now are. Visualize a specific outcome that you would like to get from this change, and imagine that it has already been achieved.

Quick Tip 29 Use all the rooms in your house

In spite of the fact that she lived in a small apartment, Gloria had shut off one of her rooms and only used it for storage. This created an imbalance in the energy in her home, because all activity was squeezed into one room while the space beside it was mostly empty and never used. A more serious problem was that the room Gloria didn't use included her entire "wealth" *gua* and half her "fame and reputation" *gua*, and money had become a problem for her. Since Gloria didn't want to use the space herself, her solution was to clean the room up and sublet it to a roommate, whose rent money helped solve her cash flow problems.

Spaces in your home that go unused for long periods of time create an imbalance in the *chi* of your home, and can indicate areas of your life that are not activated. If there's an unused room in any of your power spots, find some way to make use of that space, so the *chi* doesn't just sit there getting stale. As much as possible, make the function and décor of the room appropriate to the *gua* and to your intentions.

INTENTION—As you rearrange your space, focus on your intention to benefit from all of the areas of your home.

AFFIRMATION—When you are done, make a statement to support your intention, such as: "By using this room for [activity], I am activating [related areas of your life]."

VISUALIZATION—Spend a few minutes sitting quietly in your re-activated space, visualizing the corresponding areas of your life being activated. Imagine that your desired outcome has already manifested for you.

Quick Tip **30** Clear out your drains

Is your house constipated? Clogged drains indicate stagnant *chi*. Where water has ceased to flow, *chi* has ceased to flow, too. Remember that we want *chi* to *flow* through our homes, not just sit there.

Drains carry away waste water. When your drains are clogged or slow, energetic contamination slowly accumulates in your home and in your life instead of being washed away. Household systems that don't drain properly are symbolic of difficulty letting go or getting rid of people, situations or things you no longer want or need in your life. Take a look at what *gua* any poorly functioning drains are in, and think about how that clogged energy could be affecting you and your family.

If your drains aren't flowing smoothly, it's time for Liquid Plumber®. Clean out your exterior gutters and drainpipes, too, while you're at it!

INTENTION—As you unclog your drains, focus on unclogging the energy and vitality in the corresponding areas of your life.

AFFFIRMATION—When you are done, make a statement to support your intention, such as: "Clean, vibrant *chi* now flows smoothly and easily here, carrying any unwanted energy and influences away with it."

VISUALIZATION—Take a moment to flush or pour some water through the unclogged drain. Visualize all difficulties—especially those relating to that *gua* of the home—draining away so you are free to move forward toward your goals.

Quick Tip 31 Place a mirror on your bathroom door

Bathrooms have a bad reputation in feng shui, although if you think about it this is not entirely deserved. The modern bathroom is a great boon to personal hygiene and comfort—just ask anyone who has had to use an outhouse in the middle of winter! Due to the nature of its plumbing, however, a bathroom can have a draining effect on the *chi* in that area of the home.

There's no need to panic if there is a bathroom in your wealth or relationship *gua* or another key area of the house. This does not necessarily mean you are flushing away all your money (or your marriage, or whatever). However, if *chi* is flowing into the bathroom instead of into your power spot, it's a good idea to put a mirror on the outside of the bathroom door. The mirror will reflect *chi* away from the bathroom, so more of it can flow to your target areas. Make sure you use a full-length mirror here, because a dinky little ornamental one won't be as effective.

INTENTION—As you place your mirror, focus on preventing any *chi* from leaking away down the bathroom drains.

AFFIRMATION—When you are done, make a statement to support your intention, such as: "Any leaking away of *chi* in *hsun gua* is now completely prevented, and my prosperity increases steadily."

VISUALIZATION—Take a moment to experience how the mirror reflects a different image into the space occupied by the bathroom. Visualize the specific improvement you hope to achieve by making this correction, and experience it in your mind as if it has already happened.

Principle 4

✽

Repaint, Repair, Renew

One of the key principles of feng shui is that minor problems can have major effects on your life. A poorly maintained home has poor *chi*, no matter how perfect its location and furnishings. Little problems and inconveniences can restrict your freedom of movement, cloud your ability to understand a situation, make it difficult to take advantage of opportunities, and waste your resources.

Depending on the state of your property, you may not have much fixing up to do or you could be faced with an overwhelming task list. Start with your power spots. If you notice other feng shui issues as you go along, write them in your notebook to come back to later.

You may want or need to have a handyman take care of some of these things for you. If you do, bear in mind that it is important on an energetic level that you be personally involved in the maintenance of your home. Look for small ways that you can contribute to the task, such as clearing the way beforehand or tidying up afterward, so you add your own energy to the repair or adjustment.

When you do repairs yourself, make an effort to be fully present and in the moment, instead of rushing through the task with your mind on all the other things you need to do. Maintain your focus, and discover that caring for your home can be a meditative practice.

Quick Tips 32-44 cover "WD-40® cures":
seemingly minor repairs that can have a big impact
on the *chi* of your home.

Quick Tip 32 Repair walls and fences around your yard

Jim, a successful corporate vice president, felt his reputation at work was suffering in spite of his good job performance, and suspected that someone was "talking behind his back." When we examined *li gua* (reputation) of Jim's property, we discovered that the outside of the brick wall along the back of his yard was defaced with graffiti—including some four-letter words—and littered with empty cans, broken bottles, and other trash. Jim painted over the graffiti, picked up the trash, and installed three up-lights to illuminate that section of the wall. Not only did he soon start receiving recognition at work, but he also was featured prominently in an industry trade publication a few months later.

Any wall, fence, or hedge around your yard is an important boundary line between your private space and that of your neighbors. Energetically, it acts like a net to catch and hold *chi* on your property. If this line is damaged, you may experience conflicts with your neighbors or a loss of energy and resources in the area of your life associated with the *gua* where the damage appears.

Examine the perimeter of your property for any signs of damage or decaying *chi*. This could manifest as rotted or cracked fence posts or slats, sections of fence that are listing to one side or another, a section of hedge that is dying back, or broken glass hidden in the grass at the edge of your yard. An exception to this might be a very old stone wall which is now more decorative than functional, in which case some natural decay is part of its appeal.

If your yard is not defined by a wall or fence, walk along the property line for signs of low (weak) *chi*, such as accumulations of trash or areas of dying trees or shrubbery. Pay special attention to those sections of the property line that correspond to your main issue.

It's not a problem if you don't have a fence or wall around your property, but if you do, make sure it is in good repair. Also be sure to take a look at the outside of your fence or wall, as well, not just the side facing in toward the house.

If you live in an apartment, pay special attention to your exterior walls, and to the walls between your apartment and your neighbors. Cracks, water stains and dingy paint are all indications of poor *chi*. If you have a balcony or terrace, the railing is like a fence around your property line. Make sure it is in good condition, and not covered with rust, dirt, or pigeon poop.

INTENTION—As you work on repairing any problems with the boundaries of your property, focus on preventing beneficial *chi* from leaking away from your home.

AFFIRMATION—Make a statement to support your intention, such as: "My property lines are now strong and secure." Include any specific *gua* in which you found and repaired a problem, especially if it correlates to your key issue.

VISUALIZATION—Visualize your perimeter forming a strong container for *chi* and good fortune, which especially nourish the *gua* connected with your key issue. Think about the specific changes you desire, and imagine them as if they have already happened.

Quick Tip 33 Repair your gate

Maintenance problems with your gate will affect the *chi* of your entire property. All guidelines for improving *chi* around the front door will also apply to your gate. Keep an eye out for any dirt or damage to your gate, and fix it up as soon as possible.

If the gate sags, any number of things in your life could also be sagging as a result, from your career to your posture. If the gate drags on the ground, the effect will be even greater, and you may find it very difficult to make progress in your life. Noisy, rusty hinges that make an unpleasant sound every time you open the gate are sending sound waves of negative *chi* all over your property.

Make sure your gate is easy to find. Use lights or colorful flowers to make it stand out. If you don't want to draw attention to your property for security reasons, you can still ensure that your gate has good *chi* while keeping a low profile. Just make sure that maintenance issues are addressed, and that your low-key appearance is neither caused by nor causing negative *chi* around your entrance.

A multi-million-dollar beachfront estate here on Maui hides behind a plain wooden wall and gate, with overgrown weeds and ugly old trash cans right at the entry. Poor feng shui at the mouth of *chi* may be one reason this property has been on the market for so long while other expensive beachfront estates have been selling quickly.

INTENTION—As you work on your gate, focus on creating the best possible first impression of your property.

AFFIRMATION—When you are done, make a statement to support your intention, such as: "This gate attracts only positive *chi* to my home."

VISUALIZATION—Take a moment to visualize good *chi* flowing through your gate and blessing your entire property with good luck. Think about the positive changes that you desire, and imagine them as if they have already happened.

Quick Tip **34** Repave your front path

The path to your front door is the streambed for a river of *chi* bringing vitality to your home. Cracked cement, frost- or root-heaved asphalt, unsteady paving stones, weeds, sagging steps and loose railings are all more than just safety hazards—they are major *chi* disrupters.

Chi that flows over cracked, uneven pavement becomes turbulent, and it will have a similar effect on your own *chi* every time you approach or leave your house. Create a smooth, even path from the street to your door, so the river of *chi* that flows to your home will be gentle and nurturing.

A path that combines areas of grass or gravel and stepping stones forces you to slow down and be present in the moment. If you frequently stumble or stub your toes, make a conscious effort to be more fully present as you walk toward your door. If that doesn't help, you may need to redesign the path.

INTENTION—As you repair your path and steps, focus on creating a safe path for people and *chi*.

AFFIRMATION—When you are done, walk along the path and/or up and down the repaired steps. Make a statement to support your intention, such as: "This walkway is now a path of grace and serenity," or "This path directs new friends and good fortune into my life."

VISUALIZATION—Take a moment to visualize good *chi* flowing smoothly along its path. Picture to yourself the specific positive changes that you intend for it to create in your life, and imagine them as if they have already manifested for you.

Quick Tip 35 Fix your mailbox

Your mailbox is symbolic of your contact with the outside world, even if the only snail mail you get is catalogs and bills. Any problems with your mailbox can restrict the positive flow of opportunities and social contacts into your life.

If you have a free-standing mailbox, make sure it is firm and upright. If you have a box on the side of the house by your front door, make sure it is securely fastened. Does your mailbox open easily? Maybe it's time to squirt a little WD-40® on the hinges. And if your mailbox has been out in the elements for several years, it might need a coat of paint.

Apartment dwellers, you may want to write your name on a self-adhesive label and stick it inside the mailbox where the mail carrier will see it as he or she delivers the mail.

If you often receive mail that's not addressed to you, that could indicate problems with *kan gua* (career and communication) elsewhere on your property, so take a look around.

INTENTION—As you repair your mailbox, focus on creating strong connections with friends, family and business contacts outside the home.

AFFIRMATION—When you are done, make a statement to support your intention, such as: "My communication with others is now clear, strong, and successful," or whatever is appropriate to your specific goals.

VISUALIZATION—Take a moment to visualize the outcome you would like to see as a result of these improved connections. Imagine that those changes have already manifested in your life.

Quick Tip 36 "Opportunity knocking"

Your doorbell (and your intercom, if you live in an apartment) affect how easily new social contacts and opportunities can reach you—and your ability to respond to them—so make sure they are working properly. If you don't have a doorbell, install a knocker of some kind on your door. Choose one that suits your own taste and that fits the overall style of your home or building. Consider the symbolic meaning of the knocker as well:

- An acorn is the seed from which a mighty oak tree grows

- A lion's head is a symbol of strength and protection

- A pineapple is symbolic of abundance and prosperity

See if you can find one in the shape of an animal or other symbol that has personal meaning to you. If you choose a brass knocker, keep it polished or make sure it is treated with a protective finish so it will stay shiny and bright.

INTENTION—As you make any repairs or improvements to your doorbell or intercom, focus on making it easy for new opportunities and social contacts to come to you, and for you to benefit from them.

AFFIRMATION—When you are done, make a statement to support your intention, such as: "I now recognize and welcome the new opportunities that are knocking at my door."

VISUALIZATION—Take a moment to imagine that you have already received the blessings and new opportunities that you desire. Make your mental image as specific and realistic as possible.

Quick Tip **37** Fix the lock

If you have to wiggle your key in the lock to make it work, you may find that making progress in life is difficult, too. Doors—especially your front door—represent your ability to welcome opportunities and to move out into the world. If you have trouble opening your front door, you may have trouble recognizing or responding to opportunities as well.

Give your sticky locks a good spritz of WD-40®. And while you're at it, take care of those squeaky hinges, too. If the problem is with your key, see if another family member (or the building manager) has one that works better, and have a new copy cut. If your lock works fine but the door itself sticks, you may need to have the door re-hung. Sometimes a wooden door has warped or swelled over time. You may be able to plane down the problem corner.

Pay attention to your screen or storm door, too, if you've got one; keep it clean and in good repair.

INTENTION—As you lubricate hinges and locks, focus on being able to respond more easily and appropriately to opportunities. When you are done, open and close the door a few times, so you can fully appreciate the new ease of movement.

AFFIRMATION—Make a statement to support your intention, such as: "All doors now open easily for me, as I quickly move forward with/toward [your specific goal]."

VISUALIZATION—Visualize making easy progress toward your goals. If there are several stages involved, see yourself achieving each one easily. Feel the joy and satisfaction of having accomplished your desires.

Quick Tip 38 Get a grip!

Are you having a hard time getting a grip on a situation, a relationship, or on your entire life? Maybe the problem is a loose doorknob. This can interfere with your ability to connect with and benefit from the *chi* of that space. For example, if your bedroom door—or any door in *kun gua* (relationships)—has a loose knob, you may not have a good understanding of what's going on in your love life.

If any specific area of your life seems to be full of surprises, and you are beginning to doubt your own judgment, go to the related areas of your home and make sure all the doorknobs are in good working order. Often all you need to do is tighten a screw. Don't overlook closet doorknobs, either. They can indicate hidden problems—or hidden aspects of the situation—that you are unable to grasp.

Doorknobs that are hard to turn are also a problem. Anything that interferes with your ability to open a door easily leads to frustration and difficulty making progress in life. Squirt a little WD-40® on the doorknob shaft.

INTENTION—As you tighten any loose doorknobs (or lubricate stiff ones), focus on getting a better grip on whatever's going on in the related aspects of your life.

AFFIRMATION—When you are done, make a statement to support your intention, such as: "I now understand all the implications of [the situation], and am in control of things."

VISUALIZATION—Take a moment to visualize that you now have a firmer understanding of the situation. Try to really feel more in control of that aspect of your life, as if it has already happened.

Quick Tip 39 — Leaky windows leak chi

Cracked or leaky windows are holes in your home through which *chi* and resources can leak away. That hairline crack in the guest bathroom window, the broken corner in the basement window, or that leaky dormer in the attic can have a significant negative effect on the feng shui of your home.

Minor window damage sometimes goes unrepaired for months or even years. All the while, it is dragging down the *chi* of your home and potentially creating cracks in your finances, your relationships, and/or your career, health, and reputation.

Take a careful look at all your windows, paying special attention to the *guas* that affect your priority issue. Any problems you find are an indication that the *chi* of your home is starting to decline. The care and attention you give to repairing your windows will help to raise the level of *chi* in those *guas* as well as for the entire property.

INTENTION—As you repair your windows, focus on improving the *chi* in that area of your home. As you take any broken glass to the trash, imagine that you are also discarding any negative *chi* that has accumulated around it.

AFFIRMATION—When you are done, make a statement to support your intention, such as: "The *chi* of this home is now srong and healthy," or "Any cracks in [specific aspect of your life] are completely repaired."

VISUALIZATION—Take a moment to admire the repairs you have made. Visualize the specific outcome you desire, and imagine it as if it has already manifested.

Quick Tip 40 — Get a good look at yourself

Cheryl had the talent to take her career where she wanted it to go, but couldn't seem to make any progress. She felt something was holding her back, but didn't know what. As we walked through her house, I noticed a crack across the lower edge of the full-length mirror in her foyer. As Cheryl walked toward her front door, the crack looked like a loop of wire lying on the floor, just where it would trip her up on her way out the door. Cheryl immediately decided to replace the mirror, so she could move forward in her career without tripping herself up every day.

A cracked mirror can result in a flawed perception of yourself or of a situation. Anything reflected in the mirror will be cracked as well, literally or symbolically. If there are cracks, splotches, or stains on any of your mirrors—especially mirrors in your power spots—take a look at how they may be affecting whatever is reflected in the mirror (including yourself!).

Antique mirrors that are mottled where the silver backing has oxidized are not necessarily a problem, but they may have a distorting influence. Take a look at what that mirror is reflecting, and what area of your home it is in. Consider moving it to a more appropriate spot.

INTENTION—As you replace any cracked or corroded mirrors, focus on improving and repairing your own self-image and/or the related area of the *ba gua*.

AFFIRMATION—When you are done, make a statement to support your intention, such as: "All cracks and impediments in [*gua*] are now completely removed, and [aspect of life] is now clear and strong."

VISUALIZATION—Take a moment to admire the clear unbroken reflection in your new mirror. Visualize the specific result you would like to experience, as if it has already happened for you.

97

Quick Tip 41 Cook up some prosperity

Your stove is an important symbol of your wealth. In feng shui terms, the stove is the source of nourishment for yourself and your family. If you are well nourished, you will be healthy and strong; when you are healthy and strong you can work hard, prosper, and get full enjoyment from life. A stove that is not working properly will eventually undermine both your health and your prosperity.

Many of us rely so heavily on take-out food and microwaved meals that we hardly ever use the stove anyway, so fixing a faulty burner may not seem like a priority task. However, if one of the burners on your stove does not work, it is likely that your life will not be fully nourished.

Apply the *ba gua* to the top of your stove. Which *gua* is the broken burner affecting? Call the super or electrician, and get your stove fixed, even if you never use it.

INTENTION—As you make (or arrange for) repairs to your stove, focus on nourishing the *chi* of your home and the health and prosperity of your family.

AFFIRMATION—When the repairs are done, make a statement to support your intention, such as: "I and my family are now nourished by bountiful *chi* and become strong, prosperous and healthy in all ways."

VISUALIZATION—As you use the repaired oven or burner for the first time, take a moment to visualize the increased health and/or prosperity you would like to experience as a result, and imagine that you have already received it.

Quick Tip 42   Fix leaky plumbing

> Julia made good money, but said it just seemed to "dribble away."
> When I asked if she had any plumbing problems, she admitted
> that the shower dripped continually. As it turned out, so did all
> the bathroom and kitchen faucets. She had a total of five slow
> water leaks in her home! We immediately made getting these
> fixed a top priority so her money would stop dribbling away.

In feng shui, moving water represents money. Leaky plumbing can indicate leaking financial resources—and that's in addition to the
plumber's fee! Minor drips from a faucet, or a toilet that runs a little
after flushing, are the kind of small problem that we sometimes don't
get around to fixing right away. But when calling the plumber (or replacing a gasket yourself) gets put off week after week, a minor leak
can become a major feng shui problem.

Hidden plumbing leaks are even more serious, especially if they
contribute to cracks or rot in your foundation, which affects the stability of your entire home and life.

INTENTION—As you make (or arrange for) plumbing repairs, focus on preventing any leaking away of your financial and other resources.

AFFIRMATION—When the repairs have been made, make a statement to
support your intention, such as: "Any and all leaking resources are
now fully repaired, benefitting my home and family with improved
prosperity."

VISUALIZATION—Take a moment to visualize the stream of resources that
was trickling away drying up and stopping. Think about a specific benefit you expect to receive from this improved prosperity, and imagine
that it has already happened for you.

Quick Tip 43 Turn the lights on

In my BFS (before feng shui) days, I once went for three years without replacing the burned out light bulbs in the ceiling fixture in my bedroom. I preferred the softer lighting from my bedside lamps, and reasoned that if I didn't use the overhead light, why should I go to the trouble of replacing the bulbs? Reaching the fixture involved moving a heavy antique bed and wrestling with a stepladder. When I began to study feng shui, however, I quickly put new bulbs in the overhead fixture—even though I still didn't use it. I was afraid that those burned-out bulbs right over my bed were having a depressing effect on my love life!

In feng shui, electric lights represent the FIRE element: heat, activity, and illumination. Burned-out light bulbs are an indication that passion, momentum, and/or insight may be lacking in that space or in the aspect of your life represented by that part of your home. Replace burned-out bulbs, and repair broken fixtures; shine a little more light on your life!

INTENTION—As you replace burned out light bulbs, focus on "shedding light on the subject" and on improving the *chi* in that area of your home and the corresponding aspects of your life.

AFFIRMATION—When you are done, make a statement to support your intention, such as: "I now bring new light, new life, and new *chi* to this space, enhancing my [specific intention appropriate to that *gua* or room]."

VISUALIZATION—Take a moment to appreciate how energized your well-lit space is. Visualize the outcome you desire as a result of improving the *chi* of that *gua*, as if it has already happened.

Quick Tip 44   Have a seat

What you sit on represents your foundation and support. (No, I don't mean that people with big butts do better in life—we're talking chairs here!) Rickety legs and sagging seats undermine your ability to focus on work, enjoy a meal, or sustain a meaningful conversation.

Uncomfortable dining chairs can affect your familial and social connections, since folks are unlikely to linger over a meal. If you're sitting on a kitchen chair at the desk in your home office, is it helping you get your work done—or do you find it difficult to stay put for more than twenty minutes at a time?

If the only seating in your relationship *gua* is a single armchair, symbolically you don't have room for a partner—replace it with a loveseat, so you have cozy seating for two there.

Is that old couch your favorite nap spot? If the upholstery is faded and worn the *chi* around it will be faded and worn out, too. No wonder you keep falling asleep there! Even if you never use a chair, its appearance will affect the *gua* that it is in. Take a look at your power spots, and see if there's any problem seating that should be dealt with.

INTENTION—As you repair, slipcover, or replace old seating, focus on providing stability in key areas of your life.

AFFIRMATION—Make a statement to support your intention, such as: "I now stay focused at my desk and finish writing my novel," or "By removing this old couch from *kan gua* I will no longer sleepwalk through my career."

VISUALIZATION—When you are done, take a moment to sit in your new or repaired chair, or to admire the space you have created by getting rid of unneeded furniture. Visualize the specific results you would like to see, and imagine them as if they have already happened.

Principle 5

Clean Up Your Clutter

Clutter in your home blocks the smooth flow of *chi* through your space, weighs you down energetically, and keeps you in the past. Clutter makes it very difficult to move ahead in your life.

Hidden clutter counts, too. Even neatniks usually have a spot or two where things pile up—most often in a closet or spare room. If domestic help keeps your home tidy for you, you may not even know what's under the sink or in the laundry room closet.

Clutter makes it difficult to keep your house clean. In feng shui terms, dirt and dust are a form of clutter because they clog up the flow of *chi* just as effectively as a glut of personal possessions does. If you haven't dusted in weeks and your windows haven't been washed since last year, that dirt and dust is affecting the *chi* of your entire house. It may sound like plain old housework, but spring-cleaning your home is a great way to spring-clean your life and get new energy flowing.

If you are tempted to skip this chapter because you dread dealing with your clutter, perhaps you'll be interested to know that getting rid of clutter is a great way to lose weight! All that stuck energy in your environment affects you on a physical level, and encourages extra pounds to hang around.

Need serious help?
My "Clutter Free Forever" Home Coaching Program includes a 120+ page ebook, six weekly email lessons and an online discussion list just for program participants. For details, visit
w w w . c l u t t e r f r e e f o r e v e r . c o m

Clutter: Is it, or isn't it?
Only you can know for sure

Clearing clutter means being thoughtful about each object in your home and only keeping things you truly love and use. Some examples:

BOOKS
A few books on the bedside table are not clutter if you read them on a regular basis. That pile of paperbacks you read years ago and haven't looked at since is clutter. Your local library would love to have them, so load 'em up and move 'em out!

CLOTHES
Clothes you love and wear—even if only for special occasions—are not clutter. Clothes that you haven't taken off the hanger in years, or that you plan to wear when you lose weight are clutter. If, like me, you refuse to give up hope that you will someday be a size 8 again, deal with all your other clutter first. If you haven't slimmed down by the time you've finished de-cluttering, pass your "thin" wardrobe on to someone who can use it now.

YOUR (GROWN) KIDS' THINGS
Things your kids used to use before they grew up and moved out are clutter. Find out what they want to keep and tell them to come get it (or send it to them), and get rid of everything else.

"SOMEDAY" THINGS
Stuff that you are keeping because you might need it "some day" is almost always clutter. It reflects an (often subconscious) assumption of future lack—so you'd better hold on to it all now, just in case. It is tremendously liberating to trust that you will always be able to obtain what you need. Clearing out all that "someday" stuff creates space—literally and symbolically—for new experiences to come in.

Quick Tips 45-58 address common clutter and
cleaning issues, and how they may be affecting the
feng shui of your home.

Quick Tip 45   "Love it, use it, or lose it!"

Make this your clutter-busting mantra! Every single item in your home is affecting you and your life. Keep only those things that you either truly love or really use. If you want to make changes in your life, take some time to go through all of your treasures and see if you have outgrown any of them.

Decisions about what to keep and what to give or throw away are extremely personal. Just because a thing is beautiful and expensive doesn't mean you love it or are nourished by having it around. Let your emotions be your guide, rather than basing your decisions on what someone else might think an item is worth.

It is always better to give something away than to throw it out, unless it's really old and ratty. Have a yard sale, and use the money you earn from it to buy that new water fountain for your wealth power spot. Take books to your local library, and give clothes and other items to the Salvation Army or other charity. Get a receipt for a tax deduction if you can—then file that slip of paper, so it doesn't become clutter!

INTENTION—As you sort through your things and decide what to keep and what to get rid of, focus on surrounding yourself only with things that have positive energy.

AFFIRMATION—When you are done, make a statement to support your intention, such as: "I consciously choose to surround myself with things that nourish and support me."

VISUALIZATION—Take a moment to admire how much better your home looks without a lot of clutter. Visualize a specific outcome you would like to realize from cleaning up your clutter, and imagine that it has already manifested in your life.

Quick Tip 46 — Make room for the new

If you would like a new job or career, a new relationship, or a new child in your life, you'll need to literally make room for it. If you would like a new romantic relationship, for example, go through your closet and get rid of all the clothes you no longer wear. Then leave that space open for your next partner's things. Take a moment to visualize how that space will look when your new love's clothes are hanging next to yours.

Clear out old relationship energy by getting rid of anything that belonged to an ex-partner. Grudge items that you are holding on to because it felt so good not to give them back are keeping you in the past energetically. So is anything that belonged to the one who got away. Keeping that shirt or jacket around won't bring your lost love back, and it could be keeping you from meeting someone new.

The same principle applies to just about any intention. Think about what specific new things you would like to have come into your life. (Take a look in your feng shui notebook and review what you wrote in response to Tip 2.) Then, make room for them by getting rid of any old stuff that is holding you back energetically in that area of your life, and clean any clutter out of the related power spots.

INTENTION—As you work on clearing out any clutter in your power spots, focus on the new energy, things, experiences, or relationships you would like to attract into your life.

AFFIRMATION—When you are done, make a statement to support your intention, such as: "I now welcome new [projects, ideas, experiences, relationships, specific possessions, etc.] into my home and my life."

VISUALIZATION—Take a moment to focus on the space you have created. Visualize the energy of what you desire filling that space and manifesting in your life.

Quick Tip 47 Move things around

Feeling stuck? Go to one of your power spots and move nine things that have been sitting in the same spot for at least six months.

When your stuff sits in one place without being used for a long time, the *chi* around it tends to just sit there, too. If you have a lot of stuff, aim to move 27 things that have been sitting in the same spot for months.

Obviously, it's best to be thoughtful about where you move things to; if it's clutter, move it out, not just to somewhere else in the house. Even if you don't get rid of any of the things you move, the simple act of rearranging them will help get the *chi* moving as well. This is why cleaning up and removing clutter are so helpful in changing the energy of your home.

As you rearrange your things to get energy moving, don't forget to clean up and dust where they used to be, too.

INTENTION—As you rearrange your things, focus on getting the energy moving in that power spot and in the related aspects of your life.

AFFIRMATION—When you are done, make a statement to support your intention, such as: "By moving these things, I encourage movement and energy to transform my [specific aspect of your life]."

VISUALIZATION—Take a moment to visualize stale, sluggish *chi* being loosened up and releasing its hold on your space. Think about a specific outcome you desire, and imagine it as if it has already happened.

Quick Tip 48 — Clean your stove

When you feel weighed down by financial worries, get out the rubber gloves and oven cleaner. Remember that your stove is symbolic of your money, so keeping it clean is as important as making sure it works properly. Don't forget to wash your burners, and the drip pans under them, too. While you're casting a feng shui eye at your stove, be alert to clutter around the stove as well. This could be:

- Spices that have lost their flavor or that you never use

- Grubby kitchen mitts that should be washed or replaced

- Baking pans stored in the oven instead of in a cabinet

- A cluttered storage drawer under the oven

- Counter-top clutter next to the stove

Clear out the cabinets around the stove while you're at it, and get rid of all those gizmos and gadgets you never use. Who knows, maybe you can create enough cupboard space so you don't have to store the cookie sheets in the oven.

INTENTION—As you clean up your stove and the surrounding kitchen areas, focus on keeping the *chi* of your stove strong and active.

AFFIRMATION—When you are done, make a statement to support your intention, such as: "This stove is a source of abundant nourishment and prosperity for me and my family."

VISUALIZATION—Take a moment to admire your sparkling clean stove and decluttered cupboards. Visualize strong *chi* radiating from the stove to nourish your family's health and prosperity.

Quick Tip 49 Wash your windows

Windows represent your ability to see clearly; if they are dirty, your perception may be muddied as well. This can manifest literally as problems with your eyes, or symbolically as an inability to "see clearly" what's going on in your life.

Pay special attention to any windows in your power spots, and wash those first. Windows don't have to be noticeably dirty; even a thin layer of dust can keep you from seeing the whole picture. If you are feeling indecisive about something and need more clarity on the situation, go to the *gua* that represents that aspect of life, and wash the windows there.

Another problem is double-glazed windows that have fogged up between the panes of glass. Foggy windows can lead to foggy thinking. This type of damage is harder to correct. You will probably have to remove the windows and have them professionally dismantled and cleaned.

INTENTION—As you wash your windows, focus on removing anything that is interfering with your clear vision of your life or that is clouding your understanding of a specific situation related to that *gua*.

AFFIRMATION—When you are done, make a statement to support your vision, such as: "I can see things clearly now, with no distortion or misunderstanding."

VISUALIZATION—Take a moment to admire how much better your windows look from the outside, then go indoors and enjoy how much more clearly you can see out. Visualize how this new clarity will affect specific aspects of your life, and imagine that any muddled thinking or misunderstandings have cleared up.

Quick Tip 50 Give your house some breathing room

Trees and bushes around the house provide welcome shade and privacy—or they could be suffocating your home. If you live with mature landscaping, check to make sure that trees and bushes have not become overgrown. In feng shui, branches that brush against the walls or roof are thought to have a repressing effect on the *chi* of the building. If bushes are blocking the view from any windows in your important *guas*, some aspects of the situation may be hidden from you.

Keep in mind that the function of the room will affect what's appropriate. A tree outside your bedroom window may be adding privacy; the same screen of leaves outside the living room may obstruct your view of the front path and lead to a feeling of isolation.

If the view out your window is less than inspiring, or your home is right on top of your neighbors, it may be preferable to have greenery filtering the view. Use your judgment on what amount of surrounding shrubbery is best for your home, and get out your clippers if things have become overgrown.

INTENTION—As you trim the shrubbery around your home, focus on creating an appropriate balance between shelter and suffocation.

AFFIRMATION—When you are done, make a statement to support your intention, such as: "These bushes/trees/plants nurture and protect my home and family."

VISUALIZATION—Take a moment to admire how the manicured greenery frames and protects your home. Visualize your home surrounded by supportive, nourishing *chi*.

Quick Tip 51 Clean up your yard and garden

Healthy plants help bring vitality, growth and prosperity to your life. If you keep a neat and well-maintained yard, congratulations; you are contributing positive *chi* to your home and your neighborhood. If you haven't done a good yard cleanup in a while, however, you might plan one for this weekend—or as soon as your weather and climate allow.

What's going on in the area of your yard that corresponds to your priority issue? If it's filled with healthy plants and attracts squirrels, butterflies, and song birds, that *gua* has strong, healthy, nourishing *chi*. If you find a tangle of old hoses, an ancient brush pile, or a garden shed that's rotting into the ground, it's time to clean up.

Think of overgrown plants and flourishing weeds as clutter that will choke the vitality of your garden. Keep your flower and vegetable gardens weeded and watered. Make a point of spending a few minutes a day in the garden so you can soak up some of its nourishing energy and absorb its positive *chi* more fully.

If you've moved into a home that has an existing garden that you don't have the time, energy, or inclination to maintain, consult with a landscape designer on lower-maintenance solutions.

INTENTION—As you work in your yard and garden, focus on making the area around your house as vibrant and healthy as possible.

AFFIRMATION—When you are done, make a statement to support your intention, such as: "My home is now surrounded with a clean, healthy yard filled with positive, nourishing energy," or "My garden is a source of beauty and nourishment for my home and my soul."

VISUALIZATION—Take a moment to admire what you have accomplished. Visualize your entire yard and garden shining with positive energy. Think of a specific aspect of your life that you would like to see transformed as a result of this improved *chi*, and imagine that the transformation has already happened.

Quick Tip 52 Clean off your desk

If you're having trouble getting your work done, a cluttered desk could be part of the problem. If you work better with things out where you can see them, make sure that everything on your desk—and every surrounding surface—has to do with projects you are actively working on. If you unearth papers and files from projects you finished six months ago, the time has come to find another place for them. Perhaps the "circular file" is an appropriate receptacle now?

Pay attention to what happens after you've cleaned up your desk. Does your phone ring a little more often about new projects and deals? Are you finally able to tackle something you've been stalling on? Perhaps you just feel a little calmer and more in control of things.

Use this progress as an incentive to tackle the rest of your office— there's probably a lot of clutter lurking in your files and on your hard drive, too!

INTENTION—As you work on clearing off your desk, focus on removing anything that is preventing you from getting a good day's work done.

AFFIRMATION—When you are through, make a statement to support your intention, such as: "I now complete my projects easily and on time, with little or no frustration."

VISUALIZATION—Take a moment to admire your clean, organized workspace. Visualize yourself accomplishing great things as a result, and picture any specific outcome you have in mind as if it has already happened.

Quick Tip **53** Don't blame your mattress!

If your back hurts or you have difficulty sleeping, don't rush to blame your mattress: the problem could be with what's under your bed. If you use the space under your bed for storage, be aware that the type of objects you keep down there could be affecting your sleep and your health.

Bed-related items such as sheets, blankets, and pillows are okay, as are soft EARTH-type garments such as sweaters. Metal objects or METAL energy of any kind is inappropriate here, and storing your shoes under the bed may keep your energy "running around" at night when you want to settle down for a good night's sleep.

Built-in or under-bed storage drawers can be disruptive to the spine and/or to a restful sleep—even when they are not in motion. Use these drawers for long-term storage, not for things you need to get at frequently, in order to minimize disruptive energy.

If you are shopping for a new bed, keep in mind that it is much better to get a standard bed frame that lifts the box spring off floor, allowing air and *chi* to circulate underneath.

INTENTION—As you remove inappropriate items from underneath your bed, focus on improving your sleep habits and/or love life.

AFFIRMATION—When you are done, make a statement to support your intention, such as: "My bed supports and nurtures me, and provides the perfect foundation for a good night's sleep."

VISUALIZATION—Take a moment to admire what you have accomplished. Visualize yourself sleeping peacefully and comfortably through the night.

Quick Tip 54 Rent a storage unit

If your home is less than spacious, consider renting a storage unit for things you can't get rid of but don't need right away. Use it for your off-season clothes and sporting equipment, or for family items you don't have room for in your current home.

Be aware, though, that a cluttered storage locker will have an effect on your *chi*—even if it is miles from your home. Make sure you are using your storage space for appropriate and thoughtful storage, not just to hold on to your clutter. Go through everything in it at least once a year. Get rid of anything you are not as fond of or attached to as you used to be.

If you already have a storage unit full of stuff, take a look at how much it's costing you to hold onto those things year after year. Is it really worth it? Set a goal of cleaning out 30-50% of that stuff, and move it into a smaller unit. Spend the money you've saved on other feng shui efforts, such as a new slipcover for the loveseat in your relationship *gua*.

INTENTION—As you move your stuff into the storage space, focus on your intention to maintain a clutter-free home and life.

AFFIRMATION—When you are done, make a statement to support your intention, such as: "I am completely in control of my clutter and possessions, and am thoughtful about what I choose to have around me."

VISUALIZATION—When you get back home, take a moment to admire how much better your space looks. Visualize a specific improvement that you would like to experience now that you have dealt with your clutter in that area.

Quick Tip 55 Clean out the basement

What's going on underfoot? Your cellar represents your subconscious as well as unresolved issues from the past. Take a good look at what you are storing downstairs, and think about what *gua* it's in.* How is it affecting your priority issues?

This dim, underground space can be a real sink-hole of yucky *chi*. If I asked you for one word to describe the smell down there, you'd probably say, "musty," "mildew," or "mold." No wonder so much junk accumulates down there!

If the prospect of cleaning out your basement makes you want to crawl into bed and pull the covers over your head, don't give up before you begin. It will only take a few minutes to find three things to clear out of a basement power spot and move them to the trash or to your car to be taken to the dump. Then, take half an hour to shift any stuff that is creating an energy block so you have a better flow of *chi*.

INTENTION—As you clean out your basement, focus on bringing any hidden issues to light, and/or creating a healthy flow of *chi* through all areas of your home.

AFFIRMATION—When you are done, make a statement to support your intention, such as: "I now release all subconscious issues affecting [specific area of your life]."

VISUALIZATION—Take a moment to admire what you have accomplished. Visualize hidden issues in your life emerging into the light where you can see and resolve them.

---

* Keep in mind that the orientation of the basement *ba gua* may not be the same as the main floor; orient the energy map to where you enter the basement from the stairs.

Quick Tip 56 Clean out the attic

Are you feeling overwhelmed or under pressure,? Is something "hanging over you" and wearing you down? Perhaps you have been feeling less than enthusiastic about the future lately? If so, then it's time to clean out the attic—or any other overhead storage space, such as an extra bedroom upstairs, that has filled up with stuff.

Attics, like basements and garages, tend to fill up with things we don't really want, haven't gotten around to fixing, or no longer need. Too much old stuff stored in the higher regions of a house weighs you down energetically. Often these items are emotionally or energetically connected to parents and grandparents. As with the basement (Tip 55), looking at the specific *guas* that are cluttered up in the attic can reveal unnecessary pressure on the related areas of your life.

If you don't have time for a major attic cleanout, at least take a few minutes to select three items you don't need to hold on to, and to decide what to do with them. It's better to start with a few things and keep at it for a few minutes a day, than to bring down a lot of stuff to go through, make a mess out of another part of the house, and then burn out and not get back to it for weeks.

> Emily had lived in the same apartment for over 20 years, and her closets were packed solid with stuff that she rarely used. Many of the things she was holding on to were items she didn't particularly care for but that were "too good to let go," including wedding gifts from a marriage that had ended over a decade ago. Emily was very proud of one innovative storage solution: she had hired a carpenter to lower the ceiling in the hallway leading to her bedroom, in order to create an overhead storage area. Unfortunately, in feng shui terms, all that stuff overhead was squeezing the energy out of the only access to her bedroom, which was in *kun gua* (relationships)—no wonder she was dissatisfied with her love life!

INTENTION—As you clean out your attic, focus on clearing out any old issues that may be weighing you down energetically, and on creating room to achieve your aspirations.

AFFIRMATION—When you are done, make a statement to support your intention, such as: "By cleaning out this space, I now relieve the pressure I have been feeling, and create room to expand creatively and energetically."

VISUALIZATION—Take a moment to admire what you have accomplished. Visualize your imagination, ideas, and activities all acquiring an uplifting and expansive quality. Think of a specific outcome you'd like to see, and imagine it as if it has already happened.

Quick Tip 57 Clean out the garage

Your car is a symbol of your mobility, independence and ability to be self-directed in life. If you park your car in the driveway because there's no room for it in the garage, you've got a feng shui problem!

If you can't open the car door all the way or have to be cautious when pulling in and backing out because of all the things stored along the side walls of your garage, you may be hampered or overly cautious moving forward in other ways. When your garage is cluttered and dirty, it will drag down your *chi* every time you get in and out of your car.

If you've been hard at work clutter-busting the rest of your house, chances are a lot of that stuff has been piling up in the garage, waiting for you to take it to the dump, the library, or Goodwill. This weekend, give yourself a break from the rest of the house, and take a few car-loads of cleared-out clutter to their next destination.

INTENTION—As you work on your garage, focus on being able to move around as in your life as freely as you do in your car.

AFFIRMATION—When you are done, make a statement to support your intention, such as: "By clearing and opening this space, I create more freedom of movement for myself in all aspects of my life."

VISUALIZATION—Take a moment to admire what you have accomplished. Visualize freedom of movement in all areas of your life. If there is a specific improvement you have in mind as a result of clearing out your garage, picture it in your mind as if it has already happened.

Quick Tip **58** Clean out your car

All right, I confess, I haven't vacuumed my car in a year, and God only knows what's deep in the back of the trunk. But I know I *should* clean it out, and here's why...

Dirt and clutter in your car will have the same negative effect on your *chi* as dirt and clutter in your home. The more time you spend in your car, the stronger this effect will be. Mindful caretaking of your car removes dirt and clutter and helps to fill the car with positive energy.

Some feng shui fans like to hang a faceted crystal ball from the rear-view mirror. It deflects any negative *chi* coming your way on the road, and fills the car with shimmery reflections. I have a bodhisattva medallion in my car instead, to bless and protect it.

Here in Hawaii, cars are dressed up with colorful aloha-fabric seat covers, and shell leis hang from rear-view mirrors. These add cheerful *chi* to the car, and lift your spirits every time you climb into the driver's seat. If you like the idea of accessorizing your car, choose something that has a powerful symbolic meaning for you and your dreams.

Take a look at your bumper stickers with feng shui eyes, too. Do they present a suitable image to the world? If your bumper art is saying something inappropriate, it's time for a new slogan back there.

INTENTION—As you clean out your car and beautify the interior, focus on your intention to keep your car clean and energized so it can best help you get to where you want to go in life.

AFFIRMATION—When you are done, make a statement to support your intention, such as: "By removing all clutter and dirt from my car, I move forward more easily toward my goals."

VISUALIZATION—Take a moment to admire your clean car. Visualize stress-free, safe driving experiences, and arriving at all your destinations relaxed and on time.

Principle 6

Neutralize Negative Influences

Dirt and clutter are obvious examples of *sha* (negative) *chi*, but there are other forms of negative energy that could be affecting your home and your life. Many of these are not very obvious until you've learned what to look for. Even the most beautifully designed and maintained home may have some of these very common but not-so-apparent feng shui problems.

In Principle 6, you will learn about SECRET ARROWS and how to protect yourself and your family from their *sha chi*, as well as lots of other ways to take care of real and potential sources of negative energy. You'll also learn how to change your luck by removing accumulated negativity from your home.

For every home that is a textbook example, there will be many more where there is no clear-cut solution. For example, placing your bed in the command position (Tip 28) may put it directly under an exposed beam (Tip 65). Chances are the home you live in has a few feng shui problems for which there are no easy answers. Use your knowledge of feng shui to make an informed decision. Make paper cutouts of major pieces of furniture and move them around on your floor plan to see what your options are. Try out one solution for a week and see how it feels. You are the best judge of whether the energy in your home suits you, and of how it is affecting you.

Quick Tips 59-78 teach you how to use feng shui
adjustments to neutralize any negative influences affecting
the *chi* of your power spots.

Quick Tip 59 Remove inappropriate imagery

The images with which we surround ourselves exert a powerful sub-conscious influence on our thoughts and emotions every day. Learn to look at your possessions with feng shui eyes, and you will discover a new dimension to your surroundings.

For example, let's say you have a print in *kun gua* (relationships) that shows a woman alone in a rose garden. It's a feminine image and for that reason appropriate to *kun gua*, and to you the rose garden is very romantic. If you are looking for a love relationship, however, find another place to hang this particular picture; it shows a woman alone, and you are looking for a partner. Replace it with an image that shows a couple in a romantic environment. Here are some common situations:

- Lots of images of solitary figures in the homes of people looking for a relationship

- Busy, angular, or aggressive images in the homes of people who complain of stress, arguments, or poor communication

- Imagery that is predominantly calm, sedate or with strong EARTH energy in the homes of people who say they feel stuck

- Homes that are filled with all abstract art, with no images that reflect goals and aspirations.

INTENTION—As you change the imagery in your power spots, focus on surrounding yourself with objects and images that support and en-courage you in achieving your goals.

AFFIRMATION—When you are done, make a statement to support your intention, such as: "These symbols of [meaning] enhance and support my progress in [achieving your goal]."

VISUALIZATION—Take a moment to admire your new imagery, and to vi-sualize the specific outcome you have in mind as if it has already been accomplished.

Quick Tip 60 Place a mirror over your stove

If you face into the room from the command position (Tip 28) while you cook, your kitchen has good feng shui. If your stove is against the wall (as many are) so your back is to the room, this is not auspicious.

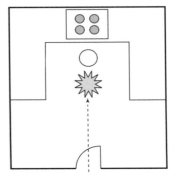

sha chi in the kitchen

Feng shui is based on the principle that everything is connected energetically. If you are not entirely at ease while you cook (because your back is exposed), that unsettled energy will be communicated to the food you prepare.

When your food does not completely nourish you, your health may be affected—as will your ability to concentrate on your work, succeed in your career, and enjoy an abudant and prosperous life. A doorway behind you as you stand at the stove is even worse—this layout is thought to lead to an increase in accidents in the house.

Counteract this *sha chi* with a mirror hung over the stove so you can see who's behind you. If you can, hang the mirror so the burners are reflected in it as well. This symbolically doubles your food—and therefore, your money.

INTENTION—As you put your mirror in place, focus on "protecting your back" while you cook and/or enhancing your prosperity.

AFFIRMATION—Make a statement to support your intention, such as: "Health, vitality, and abundance now nourish me and my family."

VISUALIZATION—When you are done, visualize safety and abundance filling your home. Think about a specific outcome you desire, and imagine it as if it has already happened.

Quick Tip 61 Place wood between fire and water

FIRE and WATER fight each other: WATER puts out FIRE, but FIRE can also turn WATER to steam. If your stove and sink are facing each other, this can lead to conflicts and arguments, especially in the kitchen.

The solution to this is to work with the Creative cycle by adding something that represents WOOD energy between the sink and the stove. This turns the WATER-FIRE conflict into a creative sequence of WATER-WOOD-FIRE (see pages 24-28 for interactions between the elements).

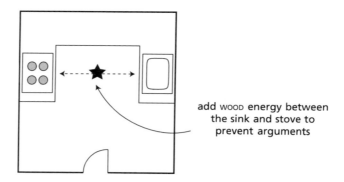

add WOOD energy between the sink and stove to prevent arguments

A wooden table or cooking island is not an effective buffer between the sink and stove, because it is not living wood. If you have a table or countertop between the sink and the stove, place a potted plant on it. If the space between sink and stove is open, place a green rug on the floor. If neither of these is possible, hang a faceted crystal ball halfway between the two to disrupt the conflicting *chi*—use red string cut to a multiple of nine inches to hang the crystal.

If the sink and stove are next to each other, the FIRE-WATER energy will fight each other also. In this case, because the two elements are next to each other rather than facing each other, it's more likely to weaken each element than to cause arguments.

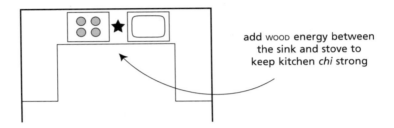

add WOOD energy between
the sink and stove to
keep kitchen *chi* strong

Since your stove is symbolic of your wealth and nourishment, it's important to keep that FIRE energy strong and healthy. Look for a way to introduce a little greenery (WOOD) around or between the sink and the stove, such as with:

- A plant on the windowsill above the sink

- A green tile or trivet on the counter or hung on the wall

- A small print or painting of plants, flowers, or fruit

- A vase of flowers or small bowl of fruit on the counter between the sink or stove (if there's room)

INTENTION—As you put your cures in place, focus on creating strong, positive *chi* in the kitchen with the productive WATER-WOOD-FIRE sequence.

AFFIRMATION—When you are done, make a statement to support your intention, such as: "This kitchen is now a place of harmonious interaction and communication."

VISUALIZATION—Take a moment to visualize the specific improvement you hope to accomplish with this cure, and picture that new situation in your mind as if it has already happened.

123

Quick Tip 62 — What to do about "fighting" doors

Doors that bump into each other when open lead to arguments. You may find that the *gua* involved is reflected in the conflict you are experiencing. Fighting doors in *hsun gua*, for example, may lead to bickering about money. If closet doors "fight," the conflicts may be hidden.

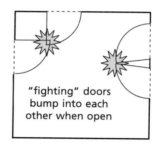

"fighting" doors bump into each other when open

Cure fighting doors with red string or tassels. If you choose tassels, hang one from each doorknob. If using string, cut a piece long enough to tie around both doorknobs when the doors are closed. The length of the string should be a multiple of nine inches. Tie one end of the string to each doorknob, cut it in the middle, and wrap each loose end around the knob it hangs from.

INTENTION—As you put your cures in place, focus on removing the cause of unnecessary arguments and creating more harmony in your home.

AFFIRMATION—When you are done, make a statement to support your intention, such as: "[name] and I now communicate more openly, easily, and harmoniously, with no bad feelings between us."

VISUALIZATION—Visualize the result of better communication in your home. Imagine specific ways family interactions will improve, and hold those specific situations in your mind as if they have already happened.

Quick Tip 63 Watch out for "secret arrows"

Sharp corners and angles send "secret arrows" of *sha chi* at whatever is in their way. As the *chi* flows along the smooth wall or surface and comes to the angle, it creates turbulent energy at the point. This can result in stress, anxiety, difficult sleep, arguments, conflict, and so on.

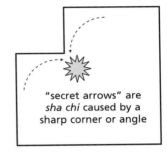

"secret arrows" are *sha chi* caused by a sharp corner or angle

Try to avoid placing your bed, desk, couch or other key seating or working areas where you will be "attacked" by a sharp corner. The guideline is that the effect of a secret arrow will be felt for a distance equal to its height. If you can't avoid a sharp corner, you can soften it by:

- Placing a live plant in front of it

- Draping a piece of fabric in front of it

- Hanging a faceted crystal ball or wind chime in front of it

INTENTION—As you work on correcting any sharp angles in your power spots, focus on reducing the tension created by turbulent *chi*.

AFFIRMATION—When you are done, make a statement to support your intention, such as: "These secret arrows no longer disturb my concentration, and I am now able to make rapid progress on [your project or goal]."

VISUALIZATION—Take a moment to visualize the specific improvements that you would like to gain from your improved comfort, concentration, or whatever was being disturbed by secret arrows. Picture the new situation in your mind as if it has already happened.

Experiencing secret arrows

Try this with a friend:

Find a spot in your house or apartment where you can stand with your back against a flat wall, with nothing pointing at you or hanging over you. Now, find another spot in your house that has a sharp angle or point—such as a corner wall that sticks out into the room, or the sharp corner of a bookcase or countertop.

First, stand a few inches away from the flat wall, facing into the room. Focus your attention on how the wall behind you protects you. Lean back, and feel how it supports you.

Hold one of your arms straight out to the side at shoulder height. Have your friend push your arm down while you resist the movement. Notice how much pressure is being asserted and resisted.

Now, move to the other spot, and stand with your back to the point or angle. Hold out your arm again, and have your friend try to push it down while you resist the movement.

It was probably harder for you to resist the downward pressure this time. That's the effect of *sha chi* from the corner weakening your personal *chi*.

Quick Tip 64 Watch your head

Jared (age 7) had trouble sleeping, and complained of headaches at night. When we looked at his bedroom, there was a shelf over the head of his bed piled high with toys and books. Jared agreed to move these things to a shelf on the other side of the room. Once the shelf over his head was removed, Jared's sleep improved.

Having trouble sleeping? Shelves over a bed can make it difficult to sleep well, due to the threat that things might fall on you as you sleep. Shelves close to your head are a form of *sha chi*. The secret arrows from the edges and corners of the shelves can cause pressure, headaches, and poor concentration.

If you're having trouble focusing at work, take a look at what's around your desk. Shelves directly over a desk can be threatening on a subconscious level, and put pressure on us as we work. Our intellectual knowledge that the shelves are firmly attached and not likely to fall or hurt us is not enough to offset the energetic threat of poorly placed shelves.

INTENTION—As you remove oppressive shelving (or relocate furniture away from it), focus on creating a safe, stress-free environment for the activities of that space.

AFFIRMATION—When you are done, make a statement to support your intention, such as: "My work/sleep is no longer under pressure; I can think/sleep more comfortably now."

VISUALIZATION—Take a moment to experience the difference you have made in your space. Visualize the desired improvement in your life as if it has already been achieved.

Quick Tip **65** Avoid overhead beams

Exposed ceiling beams create pressure over the area directly beneath them. A beam over the dining table or the couch, for example, can aggravate any tensions in the family. A beam over a desk may make it difficult to work, or may cause headaches.

A beam over your bed can affect your sleep and your health. A beam over the head of the bed can cause headaches; over the knees or feet it may cause knee or leg problems; a beam over the stomach can cause digestive problems. Beams that run lengthwise over a couple's bed can cause problems in the relationship:

- A beam over the middle of the bed causes a division between the partners. The couple may have trouble communicating, make love less often, or even split up.

- If the beam is over one side of the bed, that person may suffer while the other does not, creating imbalance in the relationship.

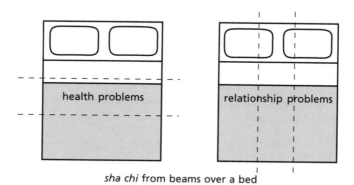

sha chi from beams over a bed

The lower the ceiling, the greater the impact will be. If you are in a high-ceilinged room, and are suffering no ill consequences don't worry about it. Keep in mind the importance of having the bed in the command position (Tip 28); you may have to choose one or the other, and may need to try both for a while to see which position is best for you.

If you can't avoid having a major piece of furniture under an exposed beam, you can lessen the impact by:

- Placing something under either end of the beam that will symbolically lift it up. Chinese bamboo flutes are the traditional solution. Hang them with red string at a 45-degree angle, so that the natural growth direction of the wood points up (usually this is with the mouthpiece at the top).

- If flutes don't appeal to you, use plants or uplights.

- Use imagery under the ends of the beam, or along the side of the beam, to symbolically lift the energy. Appropriate images include angels, birds in flight, and the like.

- Disguise the beam with fabric or a canopy over the bed

- Hang a vine, garland, or string of miniature lights along the side or bottom of the beam

INTENTION—As you correct any problems created by exposed beams in your power spots, focus on removing any negative influences affecting yourself and your family.

AFFIRMATION—When you are done, make a statement to support your intention, such as: "All oppressive energy over this space is now lifted/removed, relieving any pressure on my [affected aspect of body or life]."

VISUALIZATION—Take a moment to sit or lie in the affected area. Visualize any oppressive energy lifting from that spot. If you have specific improvements in mind, imagine them as if they have already taken place.

Quick Tip 66 Be wary of ceiling fans

Ceiling fans keep us cool and help to keep energy use and air-conditioning costs down. However, they also have a slicing energy as they spin, so be wary of placing furniture where you will be too close to this *sha chi.*

With high ceilings, overhead fans are not likely to be a problem for you. If you have low ceilings and are experiencing aches or pains, look around to see if you spend time each day sitting or sleeping directly under a fan that could be affecting that part of your body.

Use your judgment, and don't focus a lot of energy on correcting something that does not seem to be a problem for you. If you can't avoid sitting or sleeping under a ceiling fan, and you do feel it is creating a harmful situation for you, hang a faceted crystal ball underneath it, or some other image that is uplifting and protective to you, such as a bird, angel, or cherub ornament. You can also turn a ceiling fan into an energy wheel that makes positive use of the fan's spinning energy (see Tip 67).

INTENTION—As you make your changes, focus on removing or counteracting any negative influence from an overhead fan.

AFFIRMATION—When you are done, make a statement to support your intention, such as: "I am now able to study/sleep/eat peacefully and calmly."

VISUALIZATION—Take a moment to visualize the specific result you would like to achieve by making this improvement.

Quick Tip 67 Turn your ceiling fan into a "chi generator"

You can turn a ceiling fan into an energy wheel or prayer wheel by placing a colored dot on each blade of the fan in one of these sequences:

1. To turn your fan into an energy wheel, use the Creative cycle: green (WOOD)—red (FIRE)—yellow (EARTH) —white (METAL)—black (WATER)

2. To bless and protect the space, use the mantra of the bodhisattva of compassion, *om ma ni pad me hum*—represented by these six colors, one for each syllable of the mantra: white (*om*)—red (*ma*)—yellow (*ni*)—green (*pad*)—blue (*me*)—black (*hum*)

Place the dot on the top, bottom, or front edge of the blade. If you have fewer blades than the number of colors in the sequence you would like to use, simply continue around the fan, so that one or two blades will have two colors. Whenever your ceiling fan is on, these colors will turn and create an energizing sequence. Make sure you place the colors so that when the fan is turned on, they turn in the sequence you intend, not in the reverse order!

INTENTION—As you transform your fan, focus on creating a source of positive, uplifting energy.

AFFIRMATION—When you are done, make a statement to support your intention, such as: "This space/home is now filled with bountiful, auspicious *chi*," or "This fan now continually sends my prayers to heaven."

VISUALIZATION—Take a moment to turn on your energy wheel, and visualize that what you desire is already happening.

Quick Tip 68 What to do about a slanted ceiling

Chi flows down the slope of a slanted ceiling and puts pressure on whatever is against the lower wall. If your bed or desk is on the low side of a room with a slanted ceiling, you will be under a lot of pressure while you sleep or work. If possible, move major pieces of furniture to the higher side of the room.

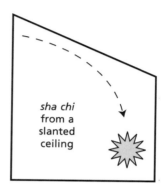

sha chi from a slanted ceiling

The height of the ceiling, the angle of slope, and the overall size of the room all affect the amount of pressure created.

If you cannot stand upright on the lower side of the room without bumping your head, the situation is considered severe.

Even in a high-ceilinged room, the lopsided nature of the space will create unbalanced energy. This can affect you in a variety of ways:

- You may feel stressed-out, off-balance, irritable, moody, and out-of-sorts much of the time.

- Others may perceive you as unstable or unreliable.

- You may experience uneven cash flow or you may have difficulty sustaining a smooth flow of business.

- Your health may suffer, or you may become depressed.

- If your bedroom has a slanted ceiling, it could create an inequality in the relationship.

If you must sleep or work under the pressure of a slanted ceiling, here are some things you can do:

- Put a canopy over your bed, or hang a swag of fabric above the bed to disguise the uneven height of the ceiling

132

- Place three uplights along the shorter wall to lift *chi* on that side of the room

- Hang a faceted crystal ball over a bed or desk on the lower side of the room, and empower it to protect you

CATHEDRAL CEILINGS

A cathedral ceiling, which slopes down symmetrically on either side of a high center line, is not as difficult, because the energy of the room is more evenly balanced. Nevertheless, you might want to think twice about how you arrange your furniture in the space, to minimize the effect of increased pressure along the sides of the room.

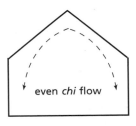

A ceiling with a flat center portion and angled sides has good *chi*, because it implies the octagon shape of the *ba gua*.

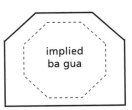

INTENTION—As you make your changes, focus on counteracting any negative effects of a slanted ceiling.

AFFIRMATION—When you are done, make a statement to support your intention, such as: "My life is now on an even keel in all ways," or "I now feel greater peace and equilibrium in this room."

VISUALIZATION—Take a moment to visualize the specific result you would like to achieve by curing your slanted ceiling. Imagine your improved circumstances—better health, improved mood, more stable relationships, or increased business success—in as much detail as possible, as if they have already manifested.

Quick Tip 69

What to do about a spiral staircase

Mary's apartment had an odd layout—three rooms on three floors, all connected by a long spiral staircase. When I met Mary, she had her bedroom in the lowest room and her studio in the top space, with the kitchen and living room on the middle level. She wasn't sleeping well (too much *chi* flowing down the stairs and pooling in the bedroom), and had trouble focusing on work (too little *chi* upstairs in the studio, because it was all draining downward).

Rather than "cure" the spiral stairs, Mary reversed her use of the rooms. With her bedroom at the top (least *chi*) and the studio at the bottom (most *chi*), both her sleep and her work improved. From a feng shui perspective this was not the ideal situation, because the energy of the apartment remained unbalanced—but it was a more appropriate use of rooms based on the energy of the space.

A spiral staircase bores a hole through your home and pulls the *chi* downward with it. Spiral stairs are thought to be bad for your health and your luck, both on an energetic level and because of the risk of accidents. A spiral staircase in the center of the home is especially bad; it will affect all the *guas*, as well as being especially detrimental for the health *gua*.

If you have a spiral staircase in your home, take steps to counteract the downward flow of energy. Some good ways to do this are to:

- Wrap the handrail in a leafy garland, or weave the garland through the uprights below the handrail

- Paint a garland on the handrail, so that the plant appears to be growing up the stairs

- Wrap a bright green or red ribbon around the handrail and empower the ribbon to lift the *chi*

- Place potted plants at the bottom of the stairs or underneath them and empower the plants to help lift the energy
- Place a baby gate or pet gate across the bottom of the stairs to contain *chi*
- Paint the steps in one of the following color sequences:
  - green, red, yellow, white, black (the Creative cycle)
  - white, red, yellow, green, blue, black (the colors of *om mani padme hum*; using this color sequence invokes the power of the mantra)

If you choose to use one of these color cures, be very sure you have the colors going up the stairs, not down them!

Because spiral stairs do represent a safety hazard, make sure they are well lit, both at the top and the bottom of the steps.

INTENTION—As you make your changes, focus on reversing the downward flow of *chi* on the staircase.

AFFIRMATION—When you are done, make a statement to support your intention, such as: "This stairway is now an upward-flowing river of *chi*, enhancing my health and improving my luck," or whatever is appropriate to your specific circumstances.

VISUALIZATION—Take a moment to visualize the specific result you would like to achieve by curing your spiral staircase. Imagine the effects of your improved health or energy or luck, as though they have already manifested for you.

Quick Tip 70 What to do about a king size bed

The box spring for a king size bed is really two box springs side by side, with a king mattress on top of them. This creates a division between the two sides of the bed, which is not healthy for a good relationship.

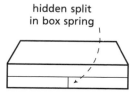

hidden split
in box spring

To cure this, you will need a red fitted sheet or about three yards of red fabric. Red is a powerful *yang* color. It seals the energetic split between the box springs to create a solid foundation for the relationship.

Remove the mattress and place the fitted sheet or fabric over the division in the box springs, making sure it completely covers the division on the top and sides, and tucking the ends underneath. You may need some help with this (king mattresses are heavy!); ask your partner to lend a hand, so you can both put your energy into the cure.

INTENTION—As you put the red fabric in place, focus on transforming and healing any divisions in the relationship.

AFFIRMATION—When you are done and the mattress is back in place, make a statement to support your intention, such as: "Our relationship is now strong and united," or "All divisions between us are now healed."

VISUALIZATION—Take a moment to visualize the mattress resting on a solid, unbroken foundation. Imagine the positive changes that will result in your current or future relationship, as if they have already happened.

Quick Tip 71 Avoid sha chi while sleeping

What's on the other side of the wall behind the head of your bed? A toilet, stove, fuse box, or major appliance on the other side of the wall will bombard you with *sha chi* throughout the night and can have a detrimental affect on your health.

In traditional feng shui, a toilet or stove on the other side of the wall is thought to lead to poor health. A toilet (or, to a lesser degree, a sink or shower drain) has a very draining energy, and any kind of waste-water carries negative *chi*. A stove's strong *yang* (FIRE) energy conflicts with the *yin* nature of sleep. Contemporary feng shui also advises against sleeping with a strong electro-magnetic field around your head, such as might be created by a refrigerator, fuse box, or air-conditioner.

INTENTION—As you move your furniture away from *sha chi*, focus on avoiding the unhealthy influence of any harmful energies.

AFFIRMATION—When you are done, make a statement to support your intention, such as: "The harmful influences of EMF radiation from the fuse box are no longer affecting me and I am regaining my health."

VISUALIZATION—Take a moment to visualize your desired outcome, such as a more restful sleep or a specific health improvement, and imagine that it has already been accomplished.

BAU-BIOLOGIE

The science of bau-biologie ("house biology") examines the effects of electro-magnetic fields on human health and well-being, as well as building material sensitivities and related fields of study. For more on healthy homes, go to the "Links & Resources" pages at www.fastfengshui.com *and follow the links to bau-biologie sites.*

Quick Tip 72 Why you shouldn't work in the bedroom

A home office in the bedroom brings *yang* (active) energy into what should be a *yin* (passive) space. This can have an adverse affect on your sleep. Plus, since your desk is probably squeezed into a corner, you're not in the command position while working (Tip 28). And if you can get your desk into the command position, where does that leave the bed?

Another problem is that if you are trying to work in the bedroom you may be tempted to take a nap instead, since the bed's right there. While this is not a bad idea if you are as sleep-deprived as many people these days, it won't help you to get your work done.

A home office in the kitchen or dining room is not ideal, either, but these locations are preferable to the bedroom. If you have no other alternative, and must have your office in the bedroom, use a screen or curtain to disguise that space at night. If nothing else, turn off all office equipment, and drape a piece of fabric over it at night, so you won't be reminded of work when you climb into bed.

INTENTION—As you move or adjust your home office, focus on enhancing your work and resting hours through a more appropriate use of space.

AFFIRMATION—When you are done, make a statement to support your intention, such as: "My sleep is no longer disturbed by thoughts of work."

VISUALIZATION—Take a few moments to experience the difference in the energy of your bedroom. Visualize enjoying more productive work and/or better rest, as appropriate to your situation.

Quick Tip 73 Why you shouldn't work out in the bedroom

Bill exercised on a rowing machine in his bedroom. He said it was a great way to work out his frustrations, some of which came from feeling that he "couldn't seem to make progress" in his romantic relationship. Given Bill's choice of words, and the fact that a rowing machine takes a lot of effort but doesn't go anywhere, I suggested relocating his workouts to another part of the house. Bill agreed, and several weeks later reported that he was feeling less frustrated and that he and his partner had been able to talk through some issues.

If you keep your tennis racket, treadmill, or other workout gear in the bedroom, you may feel worn out and tired all the time. Besides, just how hard do you want to have to "work at" your relationship? If you absolutely do not have any other space but your bedroom in which to work out, try to find some way to store or disguise your exercise equipment so it isn't the first thing you see in the morning and the last thing you see at night. As convenient as it may seem, storing your exercise equipment under the bed is not an appropriate solution. (See Tip 53 for more on under-bed storage.)

INTENTION—As you move your workout gear, focus on creating a more positive and appropriate environment in your bedroom.

AFFIRMATION—When you are done, make a statement to support your intention, such as: "My bedroom is now a place of rest and tranquility," or "My relationship with [person] is now progressing effortlessly."

VISUALIZATION—Take a moment to relax in your bedroom and visualize a specific outcome resulting from this change.

Quick Tip 74 — Why you shouldn't watch TV in the bedroom

What would you rather do with your partner at the end of the day: watch the idiot box, or snuggle? Of course, if you really want to avoid your partner, turning on the TV every night when you get into bed is a great way to accomplish that.*

If you're single, this still applies to you. If you're in the habit of watching TV before bed, do it in the living room or den. Keep the sleeping room for sleeping, and leave energetic space there for someone else to come in and keep you entertained in the evenings.

If you can't (or won't) take the television out of the bedroom, at least cover it up somehow. Now you have an excuse to get that armoire you've been dreaming about.

INTENTION—As you move the TV out of your bedroom, focus on creating an atmosphere that is more conducive to rest and/or communication.

AFFIRMATION—When you are done, make a statement to support your intention, such as: "My partner and I are now able to connect without commercial interruptions."

VISUALIZATION—Take a moment to relax on your bed and visualize clearer communication and a better relationship with your partner. Focus on a specific outcome you would like to achieve, and imagine that it has already happened.

---

* Soon after I wrote this, I was watching The Tonight Show (in the living room of course—there's no TV in *my* bedroom), and was pleased to hear Jay Leno and his celebrity guest agree that removing the TV from the bedroom is one key to a successful marriage. Way to go, Jay!

Quick Tip 75 Air out your house

Could your life use a breath of fresh air? Well, when was the last time you really aired out your house? If the air in your house is stale, the energy will be, too.

A quick way to get a change of *chi* into your home is to open all your windows and doors and leave them open for at least 15 minutes. (Even if your home is well ventilated, this is a good thing to do if you have been having a run of bad luck.)

The best time to do this is between 11 PM and 1 AM, when the *chi* of the day is shifting; you can use that energetic shift to change the *chi* in your house. You don't have to open every window all the way; an inch or two will do. If you can do this when the air is clear and fresh-smelling and there is a gentle breeze, that's even better.

While you're at it, this would be a great time to sweep out the place, and maybe deal with some more of your clutter!

INTENTION—As you go around the house to open all your windows (and again when you close them), focus on inviting new positive *chi* to fill your home and change your luck.

AFFIRMATION—When you are done, make a statement to support your intention, such as: "My home is now filled with beneficial *chi* that helps change my luck and improve my life," or "With this change of *chi*, my luck is now changing for the better."

VISUALIZATION—After you have opened all the windows, take a moment to sit quietly in the center of your home and visualize the shift in *chi*. Imagine all the old stale *chi* flowing out, and new vital *chi* flowing in.

Quick Tip 76 Steam-clean your carpets

Carpets don't just collect dust and dog hair, they also soak up a lot of grubby *chi*. If you haven't had your carpets steam-cleaned in a while, consider doing so now—or as soon as you've dealt with your clutter! Rent a carpet-steamer for a day, or have a professional service come in and do it for you.

If you don't have wall-to-wall carpets, arrange to have your area rugs cleaned. Antique rugs can be beautiful, but there's a good chance that they are carrying a lot of really old, stale, *chi*. If professional rug cleaning is beyond your budget, do a thorough vacuuming yourself.

Cleaning your carpets is especially important if you have lived in the same home for a long time, or if you live in a rented apartment that is filled with the previous tenants' *chi*. It's an effective way to get rid of old, stale, or unpleasant *chi* that you don't need clinging to your life.

Take a good look at your draperies, too, and your upholstered furniture—it might be a good idea to have them cleaned as well.

When my boyfriend and I first walked into our home on Maui, we knew immediately that it was where we wanted to live. We loved the large lanai, the wall of windows in the living room, and the awe-inspiring view. But even though it is a much nicer space than the others we'd look at, the whole place felt dull and flat. The landlord agreed to have the carpets steam-cleaned before we moved in, and we signed the lease.

Three days later when we came back, the difference in the *chi* of the space was amazing. All the old energetic crud of past tenants had been cleaned away, and we felt much more comfortable about moving into our new, re-energized home.

INTENTION—As you clean your carpets, or arrange for a professional carpet cleaning service to do so, focus on removing all old, stale energy from your space.

AFFIRMATION—When your carpets are clean, make a statement to support your intention, such as: "All stale, stagnant *chi* has been cleared away, and my home is now filled with clean, bright energy."

VISUALIZATION—Take a moment to admire your clean carpets. Visualize that all stale, dirty energy in the room/home is gone, and has been replaced with fresh, clean *chi*. Think of a specific life improvement that you would like to experience as a result of removing all that old *chi*, and imagine that it has already manifested for you.

SPACE CLEARING

For a more thorough energetic cleaning of your home, a space-clearing ceremony may be in order. This specialized practice for getting rid of negative chi is outside the scope of this book, so if you are interested in learning more about space clearing or would like to find out if you need it, check the Resources pages in the back of the book. You can also visit www.fastfengshui.com *for links to space-clearing practitioner and trainer sites.*

Quick Tip 77 Citrus absorbs negativity

This orange peel cure removes stale or negative *chi* from your home. Buy fresh oranges for this cure, rather than using any you already have in the house.

1. Peel three fresh oranges, and tear each peel into nine pieces (for a total of 27 pieces). Place the pieces in a large bowl and add about a cup of bottled or filtered water.

2. Standing in the center of each room, dip your fingers in the orange-scented water and flick some of it in all directions using the "dispelling mudra" (see page 32). At the same time, visualize negative *chi* being dispersed and repeat the mantra *om mani padme hum* nine times.

3. Take a piece of orange peel and break off little bits, scattering them all around the sides of the room, and repeat in each room of the house. If there is orange peel and water left over, place the bowl in the center of the house until you are ready for Step 4.

4. Leave the orange peel for 24 hours. It will absorb negative *chi*, which you can then easily remove from your space as you sweep or vacuum up the bits of orange peel and throw them away.

INTENTION—As you prepare and use this cure, focus on removing negative energy from your home.

AFFIRMATION—When you are done, make a statement to support your intention, such as: "All negative *chi* is now effectively removed from this space and can no longer affect me or my family."

VISUALIZATION—As you flick the water around and scatter the pieces of orange peel, visualize all negative energy being absorbed by the orange peels. As you vacuum or sweep them up the next day, visualize sweeping up and discarding all negative energy.

Quick Tip 78 Cheer up your chi with fresh flowers

Fresh, fragrant flowers can lift flagging spirits and sagging *chi*. If there has been a lot of sadness in your home lately—or you need a change of luck—try this method for bringing joy and good fortune back into the home:

Day 1: Place a bouquet of fresh, fragrant flowers in a vase in a power spot in your living room, and leave it there for three days. Change the water daily, so it stays fresh.

Day 4: Place a bouquet of a *different* variety of fresh, fragrant flowers in a vase in a power spot in your bedroom. Leave it in place for three days, changing the water daily. (If the flowers in the living room are still fresh, they can remain in place; check them daily and remove any that are beginning to wilt.)

Day 7: Place a bouquet of a third variety of fresh, fragrant flowers in a vase in a power spot in your kitchen. Leave it in place for three days, changing the water daily. (If any of the flowers in the living room and bedroom are still fresh, they can remain in place; check them daily and remove any that are beginning to wilt.)

Repeat this cycle twice more, so you are bringing in a total of nine bouquets of fragrant flowers every three days over a period of 27 days. It is essential to use *fragrant* flowers. Although you should not use the same variety of flowers twice in a row, you can repeat varieties over the 27 days.

Take a few moments at least once a day throughout the 27 days to focus on your intention, visualize the desired change, and repeat your affirmation.

INTENTION—As you place each bouquet in a vase and each vase in its place, focus on bringing joyful new *chi* into your home.

AFFIRMATION—When you have placed the vase in an appropriate spot, make a statement to support your intention, such as: "Joy and happiness now come to fill my home and my heart."

VISUALIZATION—Take a moment to admire the natural beauty of your flowers and to enjoy their delightful aroma. Visualize their glorious fragrance lifting the *chi* of your home.

THE PROBLEM WITH DRIED FLOWERS

Many people like dried flower arrangements, and wonder if they can be used as feng shui cures. Although dried flowers can be attractive, and have the advantage of not wilting or needing to have their water changed, they don't have the powerful living chi of a fresh flower. Dried flowers are dead plants from which all vitality is gone.

Silk or other life-like artificial flowers are preferred over dried flowers in feng shui. If you don't have a local source for good-quality fake flowers and plants, check the Resources pages at the end of the book to get a copy of the Petals catalog. They have a glorious selection of "life-like" green plants, flowers, wreaths, garlands, and the like.

If you have dried flower arrangements that you truly love and don't want to get rid of, be thoughtful about where you place them, and use live plants instead in your power spots.

Principle 7

Activate Your Power Spots

Activating your power spots with traditional feng shui enhancements and personal symbols is the part of feng shui where you really get to use your creativity.

Often the most effective enhancement is something you already own, and all you have to do is move it into a more appropriate spot. If you're shopping for new objects and artwork, make sure you don't end up bringing a lot of feng shui clutter into your home. Remember to keep it simple, and focus on activating your power spots before working on secondary areas.

You may have flipped ahead to this chapter because it looks like the most fun part of the book. Please be aware that if you have skipped the previous principles you could be overlooking significant feng shui problems affecting your home and your life. If this is so, any feng shui enhancements you put into place may activate underlying problems, instead of enhancing your power spots.

Be sure to identify and address maintenance issues (Principles 3-5) and other causes of *sha* (negative) *chi* that could be affecting your home (Principle 6) instead of just relying on enhancements.

Quick Tips 79-96 teach you effective ways to enhance and activate each *gua* of your home with traditional feng shui cures as well as by using personal symbols and images.

Quick Tip 79 Create your own ceremonies

Bring a sense of the sacred to your feng shui practice with a ritual or ceremony to accompany the activation of your power spots. You can place your feng shui enhancements as part of a ceremony, or perform a ritual after the enhancements are in place. Perform your ritual for 3, 9, or 27 days for best effect. If your initial ceremony is an elaborate one, you may want to simplify your follow-up rituals by just repeating a few key actions on the subsequent days.

INGREDIENTS FOR A FENG SHUI CEREMONY

Here are some things you can include in your ceremony or ritual. You may want to create or embellish a home altar with some of the following items and leave them in place for 3, 9, or 27 days—or permanently.

- A piece of gorgeous brocade, silk, satin, or velvet cloth
- Votive candles, saints candles
- Incense
- Bells
- Fresh flowers (remove as soon as they start to wilt)
- Coins or paper currency (roll paper money into a cylinder and tie with a red ribbon; coins should be in multiples of 3 or 9)
- Religious symbols, images, or statues
- Photographs of people significant to you
- Small red envelopes (to hold written wishes or blessings)
- Water, wine, or spirits
- Music
- Uncooked rice (a few grains or a small bowl full)
- Natural crystals
- Other objects from nature (feathers, rocks, shells, etc.)
- Personal power objects or mementos

BASIC PROCEDURE

Ring a bell to begin and end your ceremony. Build the core of your ritual around the three steps of the empowerment process:

1. Use the power of **body**—Perform a physical action such as lighting a candle, placing a flower in a vase, writing a wish on a slip of paper and putting it into a red envelope, or holding a specific *mudra* (hand gesture) for a few moments.

2. Use the power of **speech**—Say a prayer, sing a hymn, chant a *mantra* (such as *om mani padme hum*), or state your wishes aloud.

3. Use the power of **mind**—Focus on a specific intention or desire, or imagine your home (or a specific *gua*) filled with golden light and infinite blessings; feel as though all your desires have been fulfilled, so that your heart is full and joyful.

SUCCESS TIPS

-   Make sure you have all of the items you need at hand.

-   Choose a quiet time when you are not likely to be distracted or interrupted, and when you won't feel rushed.

-   Invite other family members to perform the ceremony with you, if appropriate.

-   Go with the flow: if you feel moved to add something new in the middle of the ceremony (or to skip something you had planned to do), honor that feeling; allow yourself to be spontaneous.

-   Take your ritual or ceremony seriously, without becoming rigid or uptight about it; you are blessing and celebrating your home, so be expansive in spirit! Dancing, singing, and joyful laughter are just as appropriate as quiet contemplation, so do whatever feels right for you.

149

Quick Tip **80** Use cures that have personal meaning

You will probably want to use some traditional feng shui cures, such as wind chimes, faceted crystal balls, or a water fountain to enhance your power spots. Before shopping for feng shui cures, take a look at what you already have. Items with personal meaning for you are very effective feng shui enhancements, and by now you should have cleared out enough clutter so that what's left are things you really treasure.

Think about the element associated with the *gua* you are enhancing. What element feeds it? What elements could you add to establish a Creative cycle of energy? What colors, shapes, and imagery are associated with those elements? Look through your things for items with these qualities.

Pay attention to the symbolic imagery of your things as well. Look for objects and pictures that evoke appropriate associations for the *gua* you are enhancing. What represents prosperity or success to you? What images make you feel balanced and calm, or strong and successful, or loved and supported? What images represent creative fulfillment for you, a happy family life, deep contentment and inner peace?

Look around; often you'll find you already have a perfect object or image and all you have to do is move it to a more effective spot.

As you look for personal enhancements to place in your power spots, keep the feng shui power numbers of three and nine in mind. If you are adding METAL energy to a *gua*, for example, you might create a grouping of three ornamental brass boxes on a side table. If you are working on relationships, two will also be a powerful number for you. Use two red candles, rather than just one, to bring fire energy to *kun gua* (relationships). Eight-sided objects are also considered auspicious, because their shape invokes the entire *ba gua*.

A side benefit of going through your things from a feng shui perspecive is that you are likely to also come across things that have old or inappropriate energy. Use this as an opportunity to clear out a little more clutter while you're at it!

Quick Tip 81 Use powerful, positive imagery

The first image you see when you enter your home is very important energetically, so make it something good!* Spend some time exploring the different symbolisms in the pictures that you choose to inspire you, and make sure that they are positive and encouraging.

A dramatic photograph of someone scaling a mountain peak may be inspirational, but climbing mountains is also difficult and dangerous. Do you want your accomplishments to be "hard-won"? On the other hand, if you are a climber, or your dream vacation is to go mountaineering in Nepal, this image would be appropriate for you. Symbolism is extremely personal, and only you can make the final judgment.

Choose powerful and appropriate images as the first thing you see when you enter the rooms that are located in (or which contain) your power spots. If you want to attract a new relationship, make sure that a romantic image is the first thing you see. If you are working on career and recognition, a mirror is a good choice, and so on. The same principle applies to other major rooms in your home.

INTENTION—As you select powerful and appropriate imagery for the important focal points in your home, focus on filling your space with energy that moves you toward your goals.

AFFIRMATION—When you are done, make a statement to support your intention, such as: "This image of [meaning] empowers/reminds me to [action or attitude] every day."

VISUALIZATION—Take a moment to visualize the specific effects of this positive *chi* affecting the appropriate aspects of your life. Imagine your desired results as if they have already happened.

---

* This is why it's not a good idea to go in and out through the back door or the garage all the time—especially if you pass by garbage pails, recycling bins, and dirty laundry every time you do so. Re-read Tip 20, and make an effort to use your front door more often.

Quick Tip 82 Activate chi with flags and mobiles

Colorful flags fluttering in the breeze are a great way to stir up *chi*. If you have an exterior power spot, consider activating it with a flag, banner or whirly-gig. Flag poles, tree branches, eaves, and porch columns can all carry a flag or windsock.

Choose shapes and colors based on the elements you are working with. Triangular flags have FIRE energy, so choose a square shape instead if you want to strengthen WOOD or METAL.

Mobiles and whirly-gigs can also be used as *chi* enhancements inside your home. Look for a mobile with imagery that supports your intentions; angels or stars are always good for blessing a space, for example.

Check home and toy stores as well as feng shui suppliers for wind-powered *chi*-activators that appeal to you. If you use this type of cure in a place where there is not much air current, set it in motion manually from time to time as you walk by.

INTENTION—As you hang your *chi* activators, focus on lifting the *chi* of that *gua* and of the related areas of your life.

AFFIRMATION—When you are done, make a statement to support your intention, such as: "My efforts at work are now attracting a lot of positive attention," or "I am now filled with new energy and optimism about my finances."

VISUALIZATION—Take a moment to admire your *chi* enhancers. Visualize a specific outcome you would like to experience, and picture it in your mind as if it has already been achieved.

Quick Tip 83 Activate chi with moving water

In feng shui terms, moving water brings prosperity and good luck to the home. Water fountains and aquariums are great feng shui enhancements because they are both soothing and energizing.

The sound and motion of gurgling water activates *chi* and adds humidity to a dry room, helping to balance *chi*. Moving water gets things going when the *chi* has been stagnant for a while (think of ice melting in the spring). Use moving water cures anywhere you want to enhance WATER or WOOD energy.

WATER FOUNTAINS
Water fountains come in many shapes and sizes; pick one that:

- Suits the style of your décor

- Is an appropriate size for the place you intend to use it

- Incorporates the materials, shapes, and/or colors of the element energies you want to add to that space

You can usually adjust the sound of a water fountain by changing the water level. Some fountains also come with an adjustable pump, so you can vary the speed with which the water flows. Experiment until you find a tone and volume that sounds right.

Be sure to add more water to your fountain as it evaporates, to avoid possible damage to the pump if the water level gets too low. Depending on your climate and the size of the fountain, this could be once a week or every day. If you will be away from home for several days, unplug the fountain while you are gone.

If you place a water fountain by your front door to activate *kan gua* (career), make sure the water flows toward the interior of the home. You want all that good *chi* to come into your life, not flow out of it!

Some people find the sound of a water fountain distracting. A fountain is generally not recommended for the bedroom, unless you turn it off while you are sleeping. Be guided by your personal response, and choose another cure if a fountain isn't right for you.

AQUARIUMS

An aquarium can be extremely effective at increasing wealth and luck. Both the water pump and the fish swimming around in it keep the water moving and the *chi* going strong.

The best places for an aquarium are in *kan* (career) and *hsun* (wealth) *guas*, or near the front door. Combine eight orange fish and one black one, or eight black and one gold. If you're using an aquarium to increase wealth, add nine coins to the tank (chose a metal that won't harm your fish with any chemical reaction).

Be sure to keep your fish tank immaculately clean. Less-than-fresh water and algae-clogged filters won't do your fish any good, and will send yucky-water *chi* out into the room. If any of your fish die, replace them immediately with bigger, more expensive ones.

INTENTION—As you set up your fountain or aquarium, focus on activating your success, prosperity, or career advancement, or whatever your specific goal may be.

AFFIRMATION—When you are done, make a statement to support your intention, such as: "Water now flows and nourishes this space, bringing abundance and prosperity to me and my family."

VISUALIZATION—Take a few moments to sit by your new fountain or fish tank, and visualize the water *chi* bringing vitality and prosperity to your home. Imagine the benefits this will bring, and picture any specific goal you may have in mind as if it has already been accomplished.

Quick
Tip **84** Activate chi with lights
and crystals

LIGHT

> Doug had been depressed for some time, and no wonder: his tiny apartment received no natural light, and none of his power spots had adequate lighting. I suggested adding torcheres in the living room to lift the chi there, as well as brighter lights in other areas throughout the apartment. I also recommended Doug get outdoors—preferably to the park—as often as he could, to connect with nature and get a dose of natural light.

Poorly lit rooms have dull, depressing *chi*. If your power spots are dim and dark, your feng shui cures will have to work harder to achieve the desired effect. If you want to enhance your love life, make sure the lighting in your bedroom is romantic. Activate a power spot within that room—by putting a pink lightbulb in the lamp by that loveseat in *kun gua* (relationships), for example. Here are some ways to use lights:

- Put a bright light anywhere you want to lift or activate *chi*

- Use a bright light anywhere you want to strengthen the FIRE or EARTH elements, or to control METAL

- Place a bright light in a *li gua* (fame; illumination) power spot if one of your goals is to understand the situation better

- Use a spotlight to emphasize the significant imagery you have chosen for a key position in a power spot

- Use an uplight on the floor in a power spot with a slanted ceiling (Tip 68), or under an overhead beam (Tip 65)

- Drape a string of little lights over a large houseplant

- Use a timer to activate your light cure each night between 11 PM and 1 AM—so long as it will not disturb you or your neighbors

FACETED CRYSTAL BALLS

Faceted crystal balls are a variation on the light cure. Their ability to refract a beam of light (and *chi*) and send it radiating in all directions makes it an ideal protection against *sha chi*. These crystal balls can also be used to empower and activate a space. They radiate blessings wherever they are placed, and are powerful magnifiers of your intention. Faceted crystal balls can be used anywhere you want to enhance *chi*.

Crystals are most often hung from the ceiling, a doorway, or in windows. For best effect, use a length of red cord, ribbon, or string—cut to a multiple of nine inches—to hang your crystal ball. You can also place a faceted crystal ball on a desk, table, or home altar. Wear a little one on a red ribbon around your neck to activate your personal chi, or hang one from the rear-view mirror of your car to enhance, bless, and protect you while you drive (Tip 58).

INTENTION—As you add lights or crystals to your power spots, focus on activating and enhancing the *chi* of that space.

AFFIRMATION—When you are done, make a statement to support your intention, such as: "The *chi* of [specific *gua*] is now strong and active, helping me to successfully [achieve your goal]."

VISUALIZATION—Take a moment to visualize, in as much detail as possible, all the ways that this increase in *chi* will assist you in achieving your goals. Picture each step or accomplishment in your mind as if it has already happened.

Quick Tip 85 Activate chi with music, bells, and wind chimes

MUSIC

Music can lift your spirits, put you in a good (or bad!) mood, get you going at the start of the day, and help you relax at the end of it—all by shifting the *chi* of your space. If you want to bring harmony to a relationship, you can enhance your other feng shui cures by playing more harmonious, peaceful music, especially in the bedroom.

BELLS

Bells are most often used in feng shui where there is a need for some kind of warning or protection. If you are unable to put your desk in the command position, for example (Tip 28), you can hang a bell on your office door to alert you when someone enters. You can also hang a bell wherever you would like to energize or enhance the space.

Bells are rung at the beginning and end of ceremonies and meditation practices. The sound of the bell penetrates the space, and signals a shift in the energy. Bells are also a powerful tool used in space clearing rituals (see page 143). Sometimes a combination of metals is used to create a more powerful energetic effect. Tibetan prayer bells are forged from seven metals, and are often decorated with important symbols to enhance their energy.

Bells come in all kinds of shapes and sizes, with or without handles and clappers. The type of bell you chose will depend on how and where you plan to use it. Again, be sure that the tone of the bell is pleasing to you—the quality of the sound is more important than the design. If you are hanging a bell on a string, use a red cord, string, or ribbon cut to a multiple of nine inches.

WIND CHIMES

Wind chimes are made from a variety of materials, including stone, shells, bamboo, and different types of metals. When choosing a wind chime to use as a feng shui cure, be sure to get one with metal chimes as they have the most penetrating tone. Look for one with five chimes, which is thought to be the most auspicious number. However, the quality of the sound is always more important than the number of chimes. Never use a wind chime for a feng shui cure unless you find the tone pleasing.

If you hang a chime in a place where it rings constantly and the sound starts to get on your nerves, replace it with a silent cure, such as a crystal ball, or adjust the placement so it doesn't ring as often or as loudly.

Wind chimes are good to use at your front door, where they will prevent any *sha chi* from entering. Wind chimes are effective at slowing down and dispersing *chi* that is moving too quickly or in too direct a line (Tip 26). Again, use a red cord or string cut to a multiple of nine inches to hang your wind chime for best effect.

INTENTION—As you add bells or wind chimes to your power spots, focus on activating and enhancing the *chi* of that space.

AFFIRMATION—When you are done, make a statement to support your intention, such as: "The *chi* of [specific *gua*] is now clear and strong, helping me to successfully [achieve your goal]."

VISUALIZATION—Take a moment to visualize, in as much detail as possible, all the ways that this increase in *chi* will assist you in achieving your goals. Picture each step or accomplishment in your mind as if it has already happened.

Quick Tip 86 Activate chi with plants and flowers

FENG SHUI IN YOUR GARDEN

If you've got a green thumb, you can enhance the *chi* of your garden by planting flowers that correspond to the different *guas*. For example, any flower with white, pink, or red blossoms will enhance *kun gua* (relationships) in your garden or on your property. If you decide to use feng shui in your garden, be sure you select plants that are appropriate to your climate and landscape.

Garden feng shui is a complete topic of study all on its own. In addition to plant selection and garden layout, it includes:

- Creating a harmonious balance of sunshine and shadow

- Shape and placement of paths, trees, and flower beds

- Appropriate paving and ground-cover materials

- Selection and placement of water features such as streams, ponds, waterfalls or water fountains

- Selection and placement of garden accessories, such as bird baths, benches, trellises, and the like

USING PLANTS AND FLOWERS INDOORS

Plants and flowers are among the most powerful of feng shui cures, because their living *chi* brings natural vitality into your home. Of course, they only bring good *chi* so long as the plants and flowers are healthy. Be sure to get rid of any failing plants or wilting flowers before they have an adverse affect on your space!

Just as in the garden, you can choose flowers with blossoms that match the element associated with the *gua* you are enhancing. Use flowers with pink blossoms for the bedroom or *kun gua* (relationships), red or purple for *hsun* (wealth) and *li* (fame) *guas*, white for *dui* (creativity) or *chien* (helpful friends) *guas*, dark blue blossoms for *kan* (career), and yellow or orange flowers for *ken* (self-understanding).

159

As you plan where to use plants and flowers in your home, look for ways to use them in multiples of three and nine (feng shui power numbers). Some ways you can do this include:

- Place three or nine small plants or vases together in one spot

- Put three or nine blossoms in a vase

- Use three of the same kind of plant, and place one in each of three power spots

Remember that you can use artificial plants in any spot where there is insufficient light for a living plant. Avoid dried flowers, which no longer have any living energy.

INTENTION—As you work in your garden, focus on enhancing the *chi* of your entire property (as well as any specific *gua*, as appropriate) and on creating a vibrant and beautiful setting for your home. As you place flowers or plants indoors, focus on activating your power spots with the uplifting *chi* of the WOOD element, and any other symbolic or energetic associations of the plants you have chosen.

AFFIRMATION—When you are done, make a statement to support your intention, such as: "These glorious roses bring the energy of love to *kun gua*, and enable me to achieve my goal of finding a new romantic partner," "My [marriage/career/etc.] now grows stronger every day," or "The *chi* of [specific *gua*] is now as vibrant and full of life as these beautiful flowers, supporting me in everything that I do."

VISUALIZATION—Take a moment to visualize the plants or blossoms vibrating with powerful life energy, activating *chi*, and blessing your home. Imagine a specific outcome that you desire, and picture it in your mind as if it has already happened.

Quick Tip 87 Good ways to activate CAREER

KAN
Career & life path
Communication
Social connections
Wisdom

WATER ENERGY

Kan gua is associated with WATER. Strengthen *kan gua* with:

- Dark blue or aqua for walls, furnishings, upholstery and/or accessories such as curtains and pillows; black is also a WATER color—use it only as an accent color, because it is so dark

- Sinuous, curvy, irregular or wave-like shapes for furniture, fabric patterns, and decorative objects

- Water fountains and aquariums

- Photographs/imagery of waterfalls, rivers, lakes, ponds, ocean

- A wave machine, or a sound machine that reproduces the sound of a mountain stream, rain, or ocean waves

- METAL energy, to support WATER

WATER FOUNTAINS

An indoor water fountain is one of the most popular enhancements for *kan gua*. You can make a water fountain even more effective by building a Creative cycle of the elements around it.

- Choose a fountain with a ceramic bowl to represent EARTH, and place it on a METAL stand or table—*or*—choose a fountain with a METAL bowl, then add rocks or natural crystals (EARTH)

- Add greenery of some kind (WOOD) in or around the fountain, in the form of a living or artificial plant

- Add a touch of red—the color of FIRE, wealth, and success; this could be a red cloth under the fountain, red flowers in a vase, or anything red that has appropriate personal meaning to you

- For a final touch, hang a beautiful, inspiring image on the wall above the fountain, or, hang a mirror there to reflect your image in the midst of all that powerful *chi*

PATH AND RIVER IMAGERY

Some people know from an early age what they want to be when they grow up. Others of us grow up, get jobs, find spouses, have kids, and still wonder what our true path is. Or we find a path, then outgrow it.

If you are looking for your path in life, activate *kan gua* with pictures of roads, paths, and rivers. Chose images that have a sense of destination to them so they won't represent a "road to nowhere." It's nice, too, if your image includes people, so you don't have to walk down your path alone.

If you are pursuing success in—or entry into—a specific career, *kan gua* is a good place for a picture that represents that career in some way. For example, if you are an aspiring veterinarian a literal image of success would be a photograph of a veterinarian in action, but you could use pictures of animals as well.

INTENTION—As you enhance and activate *kan gua*, focus on your specific reasons for working on this area of your home. What do you want to receive or achieve as a result?

AFFIRMATION—When you are done, make a statement to support your intention, such as: "I easily make the connections I need to progress in my career," or "My true path in life is now revealed to me."

VISUALIZATION—Take a moment to admire your changes. Visualize your desired outcome as if it has already been achieved.

Quick Tip 88 Good ways to activate SELF-UNDERSTANDING

★		

KEN
Self-understanding
Knowledge and learning
Your spiritual life
Introspection

EARTH ENERGY

Ken gua is associated with EARTH. Strengthen *ken gua* with:

- Shades of brown, beige, yellow, and other earth tones for walls, furnishings, upholstery, curtains and pillows

- Fabrics and textures that are soft and welcoming, inviting you to relax and settle your energy: corduroy, velvet, velour, cashmere, mohair, and chenille are all EARTH textures

- Ceramic vessels, tiles, and objects

- Large, heavy objects, such as statuary or stones

- Lower lighting, if appropriate for the purpose of the room; turn off overhead lights and use a table lamp or candles to create a quieter, more soothing atmosphere

- Use lamps that shine down (table lamps or spot lighting) rather than up (torcheres), to enhance the settling quality of EARTH

- EARTH is generated by FIRE, so a few red or triangular accents can be appropriate. Be careful not to add too much FIRE energy, however, as it may shake things up and make it difficult to remain grounded and focused.

CREATE A PLACE FOR CONTEMPLATION

Ken gua is also the ideal location for a meditation alcove, home altar, or other quiet place for retreat and introspection. If this is not possible, look for ways to evoke this aspect of *ken gua* with a statue or image of a religious or spiritual figure appropriate to your practice.

163

CREATE A PLACE FOR STUDY

If you are a student—or there are students in your household—*ken gua* is a great place for study. Keep books, items and records related to scholarly activities here. If you are using *ken gua* for study, add a bright light to this *gua*—it will also enhance your ability to succeed in school. Use EARTH colors and materials to help keep you grounded and focused in this space. If you need to enhance mental clarity, hang a faceted crystal ball where it will be directly over your head when you sit at your desk.

A FULL-LENGTH MIRROR AIDS SELF-UNDERSTANDING

If all your mirrors are small and you have only a partial view of yourself in them, your self-image may suffer. *Ken gua* is associated with self-understanding, so it's a good place for a full-length mirror as a feng shui adjustment. A full-length mirror allows you to see yourself clearly and completely. If, like one of my clients, you don't like how you look, bear in mind that while seeing your full reflection may be difficult, hiding from it is not productive.

INTENTION—As you enhance and activate *ken gua*, focus on your specific reasons for working on this area of your home—such as a greater sense of self, success in your studies, or a more profound spiritual awareness. What do you want to receive or achieve as a result?

AFFIRMATION—When you are done, make a statement to support your intention, such as: "My spiritual practice grows deeper and stronger every day," or "I fully embrace who I am," or "I am connected with my true self," or "By knowing myself, I find my true path."

VISUALIZATION—Take a moment to be in your study or meditation space, or to take a good look at yourself in your full-length mirror. Visualize that you are feeling fully centered, grounded, and sure of yourself and your purpose.

Quick Tip 89 Good ways to activate HEALTH & FAMILY

JEN
Your family
Your health
New beginnings
Ability to initiate

WOOD ENERGY

Jen gua is associated with WOOD. Strengthen *jen gua* with:

- Living plants and flowers; use silk or other life-like artificial plants or flowers if maintenance is an issue

- Imagery of plants and gardens

- Pale to medium shades of green or blue for walls, fabric, furnishings, upholstery, home accessories

- Tall, narrow shapes and vertical stripes

- WATER energy, to nourish WOOD

Be sure to remove any unnecessary metal objects from *jen gua*, as METAL chops down wood.

FAMILY MEMORIES

Jen gua is associated with "family," which means preceding generations as well as the family group occupying the home now. If you share your house or apartment with roommates, they too will be represented by *jen gua*.

Jen gua is where you come from, culturally, genealogically, and genetically. If you have health problems that may have a genetic origin, work with *jen gua* as well as with the *tai chi* of your home.

Jen gua is the ideal place to celebrate your family heritage with photographs, heirlooms, or other mementos. A "family tree" is the quintessential accent for *jen gua*, because it combines family history with the

165

tree motif. Paint a room or wall in *jen gua* green, and hang your family tree or family photographs there.

NEW BEGINNINGS

Because *jen gua* is associated with spring, dawn, and the rebirth that follows winter (see page 18), it is a good place for feng shui enhancements if your objectives include new beginnings of any kind—such as finding or ensuring success in a new relationship or a new job—or if you have trouble initiating new projects.

WOOD imagery will be especially helpful here, as will all the shades of green that evoke new growth. Bamboo is a favored plant in feng shui because it grows and spreads rapidly, is flexible and strong, and is so versatile in its uses. Add some bamboo imagery to *jen gua* when you need to get moving on a new endeavor.

INTENTION—As you enhance and activate *jen gua*, focus on your specific reasons for working on this area of your home. What do you want to receive or achieve as a result?

AFFIRMATION—When you are done, make a statement to support your intention, such as: "Our family is loving and supportive of one another in all ways," or "I am regaining my health and strength rapidly now," or whatever is appropriate to the new beginnings you wish to enhance.

VISUALIZATION—Take a moment to admire your changes. Visualize your desired outcome as if it has already been achieved.

Quick Tip 90 Good ways to activate PROSPERITY

HSUN
Fortunate blessings
Wealth and prosperity
Your ability to receive
What you are grateful for

Think about all the meanings of abundance and prosperity that may benefit by activating this *gua*, in addition to money.

WOOD ENERGY

Like *jen*, *hsun gua* is associated with the energy of WOOD. Here the wood is mature, like a stately elm or oak tree. Enhance *hsun gua* with:

- Dark green and purple paint, fabrics, furnishings, upholstery,

- Large plants, or plants with red or purple blossoms; evergreen or fruit trees in *hsun gua* outdoors

- Money: coins or paper currency; any kind of imagery having to do with money and prosperity

- Wind chimes are a traditional enhancement for *hsun gua*

- Goldfish, either real ones in a tank or goldfish imagery

- Images of things that you are grateful for—the people, experiences, or material goods that are your "fortunate blessings"

- WATER energy, to nourish WOOD

MONEY TREE

Since *hsun gua* is associated with both WOOD and wealth *chi*, why not make a "money tree" to activate this important *gua*?

1. Place a potted indoor tree (such as a ficus), real or life-like, in *hsun gua* of your home, living room, or bedroom.

2. Every day, for 27 days, roll up a dollar bill, tie it with a 9" length of red string or ribbon, and hang it from a branch of your tree.

3. Each day, empower your money tree with the power of body, speech, and mind (focused action, affirmations, visualization) to bring ever-increasing prosperity to you and your family.

CASH FLOW

I have found this variation on a Black Sect cash flow cure to be very effective. You will need a new "piggy bank" or other container, preferably one that evokes wealth or prosperity. For example, I use a round box with a design of a bird's nest and eggs on it, which says "nest egg" to me. Follow these steps to activate your cash flow:

1. Cut a 6" or 9" circle of red felt or velvet. This will help money "stick" to you. On top of the red fabric, place a round mirror, reflective side up. Place the container on top of the mirror. A specific money wish written on a slip of paper and placed in a small red envelope with a few grains of uncooked rice can go in the bottom of the money box.

2. Place the fabric-mirror-box set in *hsun gua* in your bedroom.

2. Save *all* the coins you accumulate every day for 27 days. Do not spend *any* coins that come your way. Every night, add the day's coin harvest to the box. Try to make at least one cash purchase each day, so you will have something to put in the box.

3. Each night, as you place the day's coins in the box, focus on increasing your cash flow. Empower the box with an affirmation, and visualize how wonderful it is to have a steady stream of money coming in.

It is essential to perform this ritual every day for the full 27 days. If you miss a day, empty out your coins, wait three days, then start over. If you will be spending the night away from home, take the box with you and do your nightly ritual just as if you were at home.

4. After the 27th day, count up your coins, and make a donation to a charity of that exact amount (you can write a check). Money is energy, and energy should be in motion. By giving away what you've saved, you create a moving flow of money that continues to pull more in after you've finished the ritual.

5. Leave the container in *hsun gua* with nine or 27 coins in it, and empower it to attract a continual flow of money into your life.

Be very clear and specific with your intention! The first time I did this cure, I just focused on more money coming in. It worked like a charm, and over the next few months my income increased by over 70%. That income came from a huge increase in my workload, so I was exhausted and stressed all the time. The lifestyle sacrifices I had to make in order to manifest the money were not worth it!. If there are limits to the hours you are willing to work, the number of clients you want to attract, and so on, be sure to hold those in mind as you perform this cure.

INTENTION—As you enhance and activate *hsun gua*, focus on your specific reasons for working on this area of your home. What do you want to receive or achieve as a result?

AFFIRMATION—When you are done, make a statement to support your intention, such as: "My life and home are filled with fortunate blessings," or "My income increases steadily now."

VISUALIZATION—Take a moment to admire your changes. Visualize your desired outcome as if it has already been achieved.

Quick Tip 91

Good ways to activate FAME & REPUTATION

	★	

LI
Fame
Your reputation
What you are known for
Illumination

FIRE ENERGY

Li gua is associated with FIRE. Strengthen *li gua* with:

- Red, red, red—Chinese red, fire engine red, candy apple red—the brighter and bolder the better!

- Triangular shapes and pointed objects of any kind (be careful where you point that thing, though—you don't want to send secret arrows flying around *hsun gua*)

- A string of nine bright red triangular flags flapping in the breeze

- Bright lights, red candles (use three or—even better—nine), twinkly little Christmas lights, red light bulbs

- Faceted crystal balls—use the biggest one you can afford

- A bright red telephone, to get people talking about you

- Upbeat, high-energy music

- WOOD energy, to nourish FIRE

FLOWER POWER

Red flowers are my favorite way to activate *li gua*, partly because I love flowers, but also because flowers represent the WOOD element, which feeds FIRE. There are many gorgeous red flowers you can use for feng shui enhancements: roses, carnations, hibiscus, amaryllis, poinsettia, tulips, whatever is available in your climate and season. We have a wonderful *li* enhancer here in Hawaii: "torch ginger" grows several feet tall and has a huge red blossom shaped like a torch.

If you use cut flowers to enhance *li gua,* use either three or nine blossoms and keep them in place for three days. Change the water daily, and get rid of blossoms the instant they begin to wilt. Dying flowers are not good feng shui! For best effect, bring in new flowers every three days, so you have fresh flowers in place for a total of nine or 27 days.

STRUT YOUR STUFF

What do you want to be known for? *Li* is about fame and reputation, so take all those certificates, diplomas, and awards you are so proud of, and put them in *li gua.* Haven't made it big yet? Make up a mock award, press release, or magazine profile that applauds your future achievements, put it in a red frame, and hang it on the wall in *li gua.*

If you have a fireplace in *li gua,* display your Oscar statuette or Olympic medals right there on the mantel. Still hoping to win that special award? Get a picture of one and put it in *li* where you will see it every day.

Li is the best place to put a collage of your future wishes—how you want your life to be. See Tip 3 for details on making a feng shui collage.

INTENTION—As you enhance and activate *li gua,* focus on your specific reasons for working on this area of your home. What do you want to receive or achieve as a result?

AFFIRMATION—When you are done, make a statement to support your intention, such as: "My reputation for [your goal] grows stronger every day," or "My achievements as a [your goal] are now recognized by all the important people in [your industry]," or whatever is appropriate to your personal ambitions.

VISUALIZATION—Take a moment to admire your changes. Visualize your desired outcome as if it has already been achieved.

Quick Tip 92 Good ways to activate RELATIONSHIPS

KUN
Marriage and romance
Partnerships of all kinds
Nurturing and being nurtured
The feminine; your mother

EARTH ENERGY

Kun gua is associated with the receptive, feminine, nurturing qualities of EARTH. While it is most associated with marriage and romantic partnerships, you can enhance *kun gua* to improve friendships or business alliances as well. Strengthen *kun gua*, especially in your bedroom, with:

- Soft, luxurious fabrics for upholstery, pillows and cushions

- Earth tones and/or shades of pink, white, and red

- Soft, romantic lighting and pink, white, or red candles

- Soothing, relaxing music

- Fragrant flowers with pink, white, or red blossoms

- Details and accent pieces that evoke the energy of FIRE

ISN'T IT ROMANTIC?

If you are activating *kun gua* with the intention of improving your love life, play up all of its romantic aspects:

- Pink is the color of romance, and *kun gua* loves it! Use petal pink, shell pink, peppermint pink, hot pink, any kind of pink for paint, wall coverings, carpet, draperies, upholstery or accent pieces

- White and red (which make pink) are also good for *kun gua*

- A round mirror in the bedroom signifies unity and completion; hang it in *kun gua* or over the head of your bed, and empower it to bring you the joy of a perfect romantic union

- Images of cherubs, cupids, and angels encourage romance

- Use images and symbols that signify romance, love, and union: hearts, flowers, couples embracing or holding hands, and so on

- Arrange things in pairs: put two pink candles in the bedroom, two round pillows on the bed, or two figurines on a mantel.

- Find imagery that shows people, animals, or birds in pairs; if you have any images of single people in *kun gua*, move them to somewhere else in your home

- Write your wishes for the perfect relationship on a slip of pink paper and put it in *kun gua* in a red heart-shaped box

- Two, nine, or a dozen red roses

If you like the feminine look, indulge yourself with lace and ruffles. If your style is more austere, do make sure that you haven't added too much METAL energy to *kun gua*, as this will weaken EARTH. Look for subtle ways to add a soft touch, such as a beige chenille throw on your sleek white leather couch, or an abstract print with pastel and earth tones.

INTENTION—As you enhance and activate *kun gua*, focus on your specific reasons for working on this area of your home. What do you want to receive or achieve as a result?

AFFIRMATION—When you are done, make a statement to support your intention, such as: "My relationship with [person] grows deeper and stronger every day," or "My perfect partner now comes into my life, with perfect timing and in the perfect way."

VISUALIZATION—Take a moment to admire your changes. Visualize your desired outcome as if it has already been achieved.

Quick Tip 93 Good ways to activate CREATIVITY & CHILDREN

DUI
Creativity
How you express yourself
Children and conception
Your ability to complete things

METAL ENERGY

Dui gua is associated with METAL. Strengthen *dui gua* with:

- White and metallic colors/finishes for walls, furnishings, fabrics, and decorative accessories

- Round and oval shapes, arches

- Clean, simple, uncluttered spaces

- Natural and man-made crystals

- White flowers, plants with white blossoms

- EARTH element accents and details, to support METAL

CREATIVITY

Dui gua is the perfect place for any creative activity, such as writing, music, painting, sculpture, quilting, or any other artistic endeavor whether professional or a hobby. If it is not possible to use *dui gua* for your creative projects due to the layout of your home, you can still activate *dui* to support your creativity. Display or store your own artistic creations in *dui gua*, or keep your art books and supplies there.

To activate your creativity, hang a faceted crystal ball over your head at your desk, keyboard, easel, or other work area. Bright lights in *dui gua* encourage clear thinking and new ideas. Be careful not to add too much fire energy to *dui*, as it will weaken metal. Wood energy can help get new projects off the ground. You can reduce the weakening effects of the metal-wood conflict by adding water energy as well, to make a metal-water-wood arc of the Creative cycle.

Place something in *dui* to represent future accomplishments. You can also set up a creativity altar in a *dui* power spot with objects that evoke and support creativity. For example, a painter might place a metal cup with three or nine paintbrushes on a round table covered with a white cloth in *dui gua*, along with a vase of nine white flowers, and a favorite print or painting either on the table or above it on the wall, in a white, gold, or silver frame. Add a white votive candle to symbolize illumination and new ideas.

CHILDREN

Dui gua is associated with children—a fabulous example of creative manifestation! If you are hoping to conceive or father a child, support and activate *dui gua* with images of happy, healthy babies.

Check the layout of your home to see if it's possible to sleep in *dui gua* while you are trying to conceive. And be sure not to sweep or vacuum under the bed if you are trying to get pregnant. You want *chi* to accumulate there, so let those dust bunnies grow! If the idea of dirt under the bed bugs you, remember what rabbits are famous for, and think of your dust bunnies as a feng shui enhancement for fecundity.

INTENTION—As you enhance and activate *dui gua*, focus on your specific reasons for working on this area of your home. What do you want to receive or achieve as a result?

AFFIRMATION—When you are done, make a statement to support your intention, such as: "The perfect child now joins our family," or "I am now fully in touch with my creativity," or "I complete all my projects promptly and easily."

VISUALIZATION—Take a moment to admire your changes. Visualize your desired outcome as if it has already been achieved.

175

Quick Tip 94 Good ways to activate HELPFUL FRIENDS & TRAVEL

CHIEN
Your support network
Benefactors and mentors
Travel
The masculine; your father

METAL ENERGY

Like *dui*, *chien gua* is associated with METAL. Strengthen *chien gua* with:

- White and metallic colors/finishes for walls, furnishings, fabrics, and/or decorative accessories

- Round shapes

- Clean, simple, uncluttered spaces

- Natural and man-made crystals

- White flowers, plants with white blossoms

- EARTH element accents and details, to support METAL

HELPFUL FRIENDS

Chien gua is associated with helpful friends. A strong *chien gua* indicates a strong support network, as well as lucky coincidences that bring you connections, information, or assistance—with perfect timing.

Chien gua is not as high a priority for most people as *kan* (career), *hsun* (wealth), or *kun* (relationship). However, if your primary objective involves other people in any way (and if you think about it, it probably does), it's a good idea to activate *chien gua* to support your other efforts. For example:

If you need a new job, activating *chien gua* can help attract the right headhunter, the acquaintance who mentions someone who offers you a job, the stranger whose directions get you to the interview on time.

If you want more money, activating *chien gua* can help attract a good financial advisor, the friend who faxes you an article on a company that turns out to be agreat investment, or the person you meet at a party who knows someone who can help you get that business loan.

If you want a new lover, activating *chien gua* can connect you with friends who introduce you to their single friends, the co-worker who recommends a good dating service, or the cutie who spills coffee on you at Starbucks, then asks you out.

TRAVEL

Chien gua is associated with travel—which requires a lot of "helpful friends" in the guise of travel agents, airline, hotel, and rental car personnel. If you travel frequently, or are planning a trip, it's worth taking a look at *chien gua* to help everything go smoothly through the timely intervention of others.

If you travel excessively, and would like to spend less time on the road, *chien gua* may be overly prominent in your home. Add water and fire energy to *chien* to help control the metal element.

INTENTION—As you enhance and activate *chien gua*, focus on your specific reasons for working on this area of your home. What do you want to receive or achieve as a result?

AFFIRMATION—When you are done, make a statement to support your intention, such as: "My trip to [place] is a great success in every way," or "I now have all the support I need for my [project or goal]."

VISUALIZATION—Take a moment to admire your changes. Visualize your desired outcome as if it has already been achieved.

Quick Tip 95 — Good ways to activate the center of your home

TAI CHI
Your health
Life balance
(whatever happens here
affects the entire home)

Whatever happens in the *tai chi* of your home will affect all of the guas and all aspects of your life. This is the most important area of your home to keep clean and clutter-free in order to avoid negative influences. You can strengthen and activate the *tai chi* with:

- A faceted crystal ball or wind chime, hung from a red cord, string, or ribbon cut to a multiple of nine inches.

- Natural crystals or geodes

- Any very special personal imagery or objects

Activating the *tai chi* with a faceted crystal ball can have a powerful effect. If you are feeling stressed out, try a beautiful water fountain, a piece of statuary, or fresh flowers instead, for a calmer atmosphere.

INTENTION—As you enhance and activate the *tai chi*, focus on your specific reasons for working on the center of your home. What do you want to receive or achieve as a result?

AFFIRMATION—When you are done, make a statement to support your intention, such as: "My life becomes more balanced, harmonious, and energized every day," or "My health, energy, and well-being are improving daily."

VISUALIZATION—Take a moment to admire your changes. Visualize your desired outcome as if it has already been achieved.

Quick Tip 96 How to activate a power spot bathroom

As water flows down the sink, toilet, and shower drains in the bathroom, it creates a downward flow of *chi*. Even when the bathroom is not in use, this draining effect can weaken the *chi* of the *gua* that the bathroom is in. A bathroom in the center of the house—the *tai chi*—will have a draining effect on the *chi* of the entire house.

If there is a bathroom in the *tai chi* or in one of your power spots, here are some things you can do to lessen its impact:

- Keep the bathroom door closed

- Keep the toilet seat down when not in use

- Close the sink and shower or tub drains when not in use

- Hang a full-length mirror on the outside of the bathroom door (Tip 31)

- Add WOOD energy to the bathroom

WOOD will be nourished by the abundance of WATER in the bathroom. Since WOOD has an uplifting quality, it will help counteract the draining effect of the plumbing. Live green plants are wonderful to have in the bathroom. If this is not practical, you can use silk plants instead. Because your goal is to lift the energy in the room, be sure to use plants that grow upward, rather than trailing vine types. If you do use a vine-type plant, provide a stake of some kind, so it grows up, not down.

Another good way to bring WOOD energy into the bathroom is with photographs or artwork of trees, and with green towels, a green rug, and so on. For added effect, you can accent your bathroom with a few touches of red to create a WATER-WOOD-FIRE arc of the Creative cycle. Some good ways to do this are:

- Green plants with red blossoms

- Add a red frame or matt to your WOOD-energy artwork

- Use a shower curtain with a pattern of green leaves and red or pink blossoms

- Place a vase with three red silk roses on the toilet tank

- Paint the walls green and the ceiling a pale pink

If there is a bathroom in *kun gua* (relationships), turn it into a sanctuary for relaxation and renewal. Celebrate all the receptive, nurturing qualities of *kun* with a pampering bath: use scented or aromatherapy bath salts or bubble bath; light a few candles; set a vase of flowers on the corner of the tub; set out fresh towels; play relaxing music; invite that special someone to join you in the tub.

INTENTION—As you add WOOD energy to your bathroom, focus on using the rising energy of WOOD to counteract the sinking effects of the bathroom drains.

AFFIRMATION—When you are done, make a statement to support your intention, such as: "I feel more energetic and healthy now that *chi* is no longer draining away here," or "This room is now a source of creative energy, enhancing the *chi* of [specific *gua*]," or whatever is appropriate to your specific situation.

VISUALIZATION—Take a moment to admire the new energy you have created for your bathroom. Visualize a specific result you hope to realize from strengthening the *chi* of this *gua*, as if it has already happened.

Principle 8

Work on Yourself
as Well as Your Home

Feng shui is sometimes called "acupuncture for the home" because it opens, adjusts and balances the flow of *chi* through a space. In this chapter you are encouraged to explore ways to open, adjust and balance your own personal *chi* through a variety of forms of feng shui for the body.

While some of these methods are not necessarily "fast" in the sense that you will see best results from a consistent practice over time, they are all methods that you can get started with right away.

Quick Tips 97-105 suggest different ways to
reduce stress and enhance your personal *chi*
for improved health and well-being.

IMPORTANT NOTE

*The suggestions in this chapter
are in no way intended as medical advice.
If you have any health conditions or concerns,
please consult with your physician before
trying any of these practices.*

Quick Tip 97 Aromatherapy and Flower Essences

AROMATHERAPY

Aromatherapy uses essential oils extracted from flowers, spices, herbs and other plants to balance and adjust the emotions and for physical health. Essential oils can be used with massage, added to baths or a bowl of warm water, vaporized with a diffuser, or as perfumes. If the oil will touch your skin, dilute it by mixing a few drops with a neutral carrier oil such as almond oil. Scented candles and soaps can also be used for aromatherapy.

With the increasing popularity of feng shui, specific scents and oils are beginning to be associated with the different areas of the *ba gua*. If you'd like to explore the use of essential oils in feng shui, check out Jami Lin's book, *The Essence of Feng Shui*. Jami has also developed a line of *chakra/ba gua* fragrance blends.

I recommend choosing essential oils based on your priority issues, as shown in the table on the following page. Then, use aromatherapy in your power spots to help activate those areas of your home.

Keep in mind that:

- Synthetic oils, while often cheaper, are not recommended for feng shui, as they may contain chemical residues; they also lack the vital life force—the *chi* —of the natural plant.

- Essential oils are extremely concentrated, and are contra-indicated for some health conditions, including pregnancy. If you are pregnant or are being treated for a health condition, please check with your doctor and with a trained aromatherapist before experimenting with essential oils.

See the Resources pages for more information about aromatherapy, or visit www.fastfengshui.com for links to related websites.

ISSUE	ESSENTIAL OILS
CALMING	angelica root, chamomile, hyacinth, lavender, lemon, yarrow
CLARITY	bay, lily of the valley, peppermint
CLEANSING	bay, cedar, citronella, clove, lime
CONFIDENCE	bergamot, patchouli, vanilla, violet
COURAGE	black pepper, cinnamon, fennel, galangal, sweet pea, thyme
ENTHUSIASM	cardamom, jasmine, ylang ylang
HEALTH	amber, calendula, camphor, carnation, coriander, eucalyptus, myrrh, rosemary
JOY	cinnamon, elderberry, neroli, orange, strawberry
LOVE	coriander, cyclamen, freesia, gardenia, hyacinth, jasmine, plumeria
PEACE	apple, basil, cyclamen, freesia, gardenia, lavender, plumeria
PROSPERITY	basil, ginger, heliotrope, nutmeg, oakmoss, patchouli, sage, vanilla
PSYCHIC ABILITY	bay, celery, cinnamon, honeysuckle, iris, mimosa, night-blooming cereus, nutmeg, star anise
SECURITY	oakmoss, vetivert
SEXUALITY	cardamom, cinnamon, ginger, magnolia, muguet, musk, sandalwood, ylang ylang
SPIRITUALITY	cedar, frankincense, gardenia, myrrh
TRUST	lemon verbena
VITALITY	bay, bergamot, carnation, cinnamon, galangal, ginger

FLOWER ESSENCES

Flower essences are created to address emotional states that can keep us functioning at less than our best and which underly many illnesses—such as anxiety, homesickness, regret, pessimism, anger, arrogance, envy, fanaticism, and resentment. Flower remedies have even been developed to help offset the influence of difficult astrology.

These healing remedies are made by a process that transfers the vital energy of live flowers into pure spring water. The resulting flower essences are taken internally, either by placing a few drops on the tongue or by drinking a few drops in a glass of water over several hours. Their effect is usually subtle, but often quite powerful.

The best-known flower essences are the Bach Flower Remedies, but there are many others as well. For more information, see the Resources pages in the back of the book, or visit www.fastfengshui.com for links to related websites.

Quick Tip 98 — Color Therapy

FIVE ELEMENT COLOR THERAPY

In addition to using colors in your space, you can enhance the effects of feng shui by choosing the colors you wear based on feng shui principles. For example:

- To enhance communication or to support your career, wear black or dark blue (WATER)

- To help get new projects started successfully, or to bring new energy to a situation, wear green (WOOD)

- If you want to get noticed, enhance your luck, or feel strong and confident, wear red (FIRE)

- White is a good color for creativity (METAL)

- Pink surrounds you with the *chi* of romance (*kun gua*)

- Browns helps you feel grounded and secure (EARTH)

Let your personal preferences guide you. Feng shui principles might recommend wearing a red suit to an important meeting or interview because it is the color of success and good fortune. This strategy will backfire if you hate red or think you look terrible in it. Wearing a red suit will only work for you if you will feel confident and successful in that color. Fortunately, you can draw on the power of the color red (or whatever is appropriate to your goals) without dressing in red from head to toe. You can:

- Wear red underwear
- Wear red shoes
- Carry a red purse
- Choose red jewelry or a watch with a red band
- Wear a red belt or necktie
- Use a scarf with red accents

Keep the Creative cycle of the elements in mind as you plan your power outfit. If you are using red as an accent color with a black suit, remember that the WATER element will put out the FIRE. Wear a green shirt or blouse to create a WATER-WOOD-FIRE arc of the Creative cycle, which will enhance the effect of your red accents.

CHROMOTHERAPY

Chromotherapy is a healing practice that balances the mind, body, and spirit through the use of color. The theory is that the specific wavelength of each color has an effect on the endocrine system and the brain, and can work very quickly on a subconscious level.

Some of the vehicles used in color therapy include: colored lights, prisms, colored bath treatments, and colored eyeglass lenses. Other colored lenses can be used to energize pure water when sunlight passes through them. Drink the water to receive the color benefits.

We can have surprisingly strong emotional reactions to specific colors. These reactions are highly personal. A strong attraction to a certain color can indicate an energetic imbalance that will be corrected by that color's vibration. Other colors may cause negative feelings that can be investigated as part of the healing process. Some of the energy associations for specific colors are shown in the chart on the next page.

For additional information about chromotherapy, see the Resources pages at the back of the book, or visit www.fastfengshui.com for links to related websites.

COLOR	USED FOR	TOO MUCH CAN CAUSE
RED	Blood or circulatory problems	Agitation
	Depression, lack of confidence	Anxiety
	Fatigue	Aggression
	Pain reduction	
ORANGE	Digestive problems	Agitation
	Weak immune system	Anxiety
	Depression, lack of joy	
	Social withdrawal	
YELLOW	Mental clarity and focus	Exhaustion
	Skin problems	Depression
	Poor self-esteem	
	Apathy, lack of interest in life	
GREEN	Calming nerves	Increase in negative energies
	Healing broken bones	
	Balancing emotions	
	Relaxing tense muscles	
BLUE	Calming nerves	Lack of compassion
	Spiritual protection	Depression
	Fever reduction, burns	
INDIGO	Head colds	Drowsiness
	Eye and sinus problems	Headache
	Purification	
	Intuition and psychic ability	
VIOLET	Rheumatism	Spaciness
	Epilepsy	
	Deep tissue work	
	Enhance creativity	
LAVENDER	Balancing	Fatigue
	Insomnia	Disorientation
	Spiritual healing	

Quick Tip 99 Relax your muscles

Massage is an ancient form of manual therapy that is practiced in virtually every culture in a variety of forms, from Swedish to Shiatsu, Thai, and Hawaiian Lomi Lomi. Massage feels so good because it releases tension, loosens tight muscles, and improves circulation in the blood and lymph systems, which assist in cleansing and detoxification of the body.

From a feng shui perspective, massage and other forms of body work can help improve the flow of *chi* through your body by helping you to release long-held emotional as well as physical tension and stress. By clearing these from the body, you will be better able to benefit from the improved energy and *chi* of your home. If you feng shui your home but hold old patterns in your muscles and other tissues, moving with change will be more difficult for you.

In addition to feeling great, regular massage treatments can help with the management of chronic pain conditions, and can reduce the need for antidepressants. If you are interested in learning more about the therapeutic uses of massage for a wide range of complaints and conditions, visit the Touch Research Institute website at www.miami.edu/touch-research/home.html for database of research studies.

For more information or to find a massage therapist near you, visit www.fastfengshui.com for links to massage websites and directories.

Quick Tip 100 Realign your spine

Chiropractic is a form of bodywork that focuses on maximizing the human body's recuperative and self-healing ability. Best known for treatment of back injuries through manipulation of the spine and related tissues, chiropractic is a holistic system of health care that includes nutrition, exercise, herbal medicine, and homeopathy.

The nervous system in general, and especially the spinal cord, is seen as the primary control mechanism of the body. When spinal vertebrae are out of alignment, the flow of energy through the nerves connected to the spine can be compromised. This can result in pain, chronic tension, headaches, or numbness in the arms or legs, and affects the body's ability to heal itself.

Spinal subluxation, as these misalignments are called, can result from a wide range of factors, including birth trauma, bad posture, falls, poor sleeping positions, chronic tension, anxiety, poor diet, not enough exercise, and the like.

With chiropractic care, skeletal misalignments—which can involve the bones, nerves, muscles, ligaments, and connective tissue—are adjusted to relieve systems and restore the health of the body without surgery.

Doctors of Chiropractic are licensed after extensive clinical and academic training through accredited chiropractic colleges.

For more information, or to find a chiropractor near you, visit the "Links & Resources" pages at www.fastfengshui.com.

Quick Tip **101** Balance your inner chi

CHINESE HERBAL MEDICINE

Chinese herbal medicine is the oldest existing form of internal medicine. Because it views the patient as a unique whole, rather than as a collection of symptoms, different patients with identical symptoms may receive different treatments. According to Traditional Chinese Medicine (TCM), all health problems are caused by imbalance in the blood and chi systems. Diagnosis describes conditions in terms of "deficient," "sinking," or "stagnant" *chi*, "heat in the blood," and so on. Diagnosis includes a complex method of pulse-taking, voice and posture analysis, and inspection of the face, hands, fingernails, and tongue. Based on this diagnosis, a combination of herbs, roots, and barks is prescribed to rebalance the *chi* of the body and thus restore health.

ACUPUNCTURE

The philosophy of acupuncture is that energy runs through the body along a pattern of "meridians" that deliver *chi* to the organs and ensure proper functioning. When meridians are blocked, proper *chi* flow is interrupted, and disharmonies occur that eventually manifest as disease. Restoring the flow of *chi* through the body meridians removes the cause of the disease, and symptoms are relieved. This is accomplished by stimulating specific points along the meridians with very thin needles (acupuncture), pressure (*shiatsu*), or heat (moxibustion).

For more information, see the Resources pages or visit www.fastfengshui.com for links to related websites.

AYURVEDA

This ancient Indian "science of life," is a holistic health practice based on adjusting three types of energy, or *doshas*. Each person's health and metabolism is the result of a unique combination of these doshas:

Vata: quick and irregular; characterized by creativity, alertness, high energy, enthusiasm; when aggravated results in anxiety, hyperactivity, spaciness, indecision, insecurity, insomnia

Pitta: fast and decisive; characterized by concentration, courage, self-confidence, leadership, generosity; when aggravated causes aggression, irritability, impatience, bossiness

Kapha: slow and methodical; easy-going, affectionate, compassionate, patient, reliable, graceful, self-sufficient; when aggravated can be sluggish, apathetic, needy, overweight, procrastinating

Ayurveda believes that we are born in a state of balance, which is easily upset by diet, emotions, and seasonal and environmental factors. Disease and ill health result when one or more doshas become too weak or too strong. Symptoms of disease alert us that we have fallen out of harmony. Through diet, exercise, body work, color, sound and aroma, ayurveda brings the doshas back into balance for a healthier body, mind, and spirit. Ayurveda recognizes that harmony of mind and spirit is the basis for physical health. By paying attention to what foods and lifestyle support and balance us—or result in stress and fatigue— we can learn to transform both our immediate and long-term conditions into greater health and vitality.

To learn more, see the Resources pages in the back of the book or visit www.fastfengshui.com for links to related websites.

Quick Tip 102 Detoxify yourself

If you've begin to de-clutter your home (Principle 5), you know what a great difference getting rid of clutter makes on the energy of your home. So, how about getting rid of some of the extra pounds and accumulated toxins cluttering up your body? Even if you exercise regularly, don't smoke, and eat a healthy diet, you are still exposed to a frightening array of environmental toxins from the air you breathe, the supposedly clean water you drink, the synthetic materials and chemicals in your clothes, furnishings, cleaning supplies, and so on.

DIGESTIVE SYSTEM CLEANSING

When your body processes wastes—including many toxins—much of it is expelled through the lower digestive system. A healthy digestive system is fairly good at getting rid of what you don't want in your body, but over the years things tend to build up in there. Many health problems can be traced to poor elimination, and the discomfort of constipation or diarrhea is the least of it. Other symptoms and diseases include: fatigue, indigestion, lower back pain, weight gain, bad skin, and a host of other ailments including colon cancer.

You can cleanse and reset your digestive system with herbal formulas, colonic irrigation, and juice fasting. For more information on internal cleansing visit www.fastfengshui.com for links to related websites.

JUICE FASTING

On a juice fast, you abstain from solid foods and drink plenty of fresh organic fruit and vegetable juices and herbal teas throughout the day. Juice fasting gives your digestive organs a rest, helps to detoxify your system, and supports the natural healing ability of the body. In addition to metabolic changes, a juice fast can support enhanced spiritual awareness, mental clarity, and emotional release work.

Juice fasts are a widely practiced therapy in European spas and clinics, and are becoming increasingly popular in the U.S. as more people experience their benefits first-hand. Most people in good health can undertake a juice fast of one to three days or longer without supervision.* Contraindications include diabetes, pregnancy, underweight, immune system disorders, and low blood pressure.

Nutrition is not a concern on a short-term juice fast. Fresh, organic fruit and vegetable juices provide lots of vitamins and minerals, as well as sufficient calories that you should not feel hungry on a one- to three-day juice fast. If you like, add some spirulina or super blue-green algae to your juice for additional nutrients, or take them in supplement form.

It's difficult to do a juice fast without a juicer of your own. The best models are expensive, but adequate ones are available for under $100. Without a juicer, you'll want to find a juice bar near you so you can purchase freshly extracted juice at least once a day. Bottled juices—even organic ones—are pasteurized, which destroys enzymes and vitamins; they are not a good source of nourishment on a juice fast.

If you continue your juice fast for more than a day or two, you may experience detoxification symptoms—especially if you smoke, drink lots of coffee or alcohol, or have a long history of unhealthy eating habits. Detoxification can manifest as cold- or flu-like symptoms such as headache, nausea, tiredness, congestion, even fever. The symptoms should pass in a day or two. Remember that it took a long time to load all that gunk into your body, and be happy that you are releasing it! Take a day off if you can, and get plenty of rest. The best way to minimize detoxification is to cleanse your digestive system before you start.

For more information on juice fasting, see the Resources pages in the back of the book.

---

* Obviously, if you have any health conditions or are taking prescription medication, you will discuss juice fasting with your doctor first.

Quick Tip 103 Stretch your body, mind, and spirit

Yoga combines stretching and toning postures (*asanas*) with breathwork and meditation. It balances the mind, body, and emotions, and gives strength, energy, and clarity of purpose to the practitioner. While the ultimate goal of yoga is enlightenment, it is popular as an effective technique for fitness and relaxation. Yoga:

- Improves physical alignment of the body
- Strengthens the spine
- Massages the internal organs and improves circulation
- Increases strength, flexibility, balance, and mental clarity
- Teaches self-awareness and humility
- Quiets and focuses the mind

One of yoga's great advantages is that it can be practiced by anyone, of any age and any fitness level, with postures and practices adapted for less-flexible students. You can start at whatever level you are at and advance at your own pace. The many styles and schools of yoga include Sivananda, Iyengar, Ashtanga, Kripalu, and Jivamukti. While they all share a common lineage, the different methods vary from gentle stretching to sweaty exertion. If you have not tried yoga before, it's a good idea to do some preliminary research to find out which types of yoga are most suitable for your fitness level and goals.

There are hundreds of books, videos, CDs and tapes available, in addition to numerous yoga schools and instructors across the country. For more information, see the Resources pages in the back of the book, pick up a copy of *Yoga Journal* magazine, or check out the yoga links at www.fastfengshui.com.

Quick Tip 104 Move your chi

Qigong and *tai chi chuan* are two forms of moving meditation that are widely used in China and increasingly in the West for enhancing physical, mental, and spiritual well-being.

QIGONG

Qigong is an ancient Chinese method of self-healing that translates as "cultivating the life force." Through gentle breathing and meditation techniques, *qigong* increases the flow of *qi* (*chi*) through the body, and enables the practitioner to direct that flow of *chi* with intention.

There are literally hundreds—even thousands—of specific *qigong* practices. These divide into internal *qigong*, which uses breath and mental focus to direct *chi*, and external *qigong*, which incorporates simple body movements. Both methods are widely used throughout China to treat disease, maintain health and vitality, and increase longevity.

Regular *qigong* practice develops mental clarity, reduces stress, and supports the body's self-healing capabilities. Many clinical studies have documented that it increases oxygen flow, improves the immune system, and aids both the brain and the nervous system. In China, *qigong* is believed to be an effective cure for all kinds of illness, including asthma, diabetes, hypertension, cancer, and psychological problems.

TAI CHI CHUAN

Tai chi chuan is the foundation of all oriental martial arts. It shares many principles with *qigong* and applies them to the art of self-defense using non-offensive moves that redirect an assailant's energy. Several forms of *tai chi chuan* are practiced as a graceful moving meditation with 108 movements that flow together in a specific order. Shorter versions of 20 to 40 movements have been adapted from the traditional practice to make it easier for beginners to learn the basics, and for those with limited stamina to benefit from the practice.

Tai chi chuan enhances the balance and flow of internal *chi* and improves the body's self-healing abilities. In Western terms, the flow of oxygen and nutritional elements to the tissues is improved, the lymph system is better able to eliminate waste products, the immune system is strengthened, and both the brain and the nervous system are directed toward healing. The regular practice of *tai chi chuan* increases body awareness, concentration, balance, stamina, proper body alignment, and flexibility.

For more information about *tai chi chuan* and *qigong*, see the Resources pages in the back of the book, or visit www.fastfengshui.com for links to related websites.

Quick Tip **105** Quiet your mind

Being still for a few minutes a day lets your inner wisdom come forth. People who have been meditating for many years often discover, when they learn about feng shui, that they have already made appropriate adjustments to their space. This is because their meditation practice has enabled them to intuitively sense what's going on energetically in their environment.

A regular meditation practice will help you become more aware of your own physical and mental *chi*, and be more in tune with the *chi* of your home. If you do not already have a meditation practice, consider starting one now. Begin slowly, perhaps by simply observing your breath and thoughts for five minutes each morning.

A SIMPLE CALMING MEDITATION

Sit with your back straight in an upright chair, or cross-legged on the floor with a cushion under your hips. Rest your hands on your thighs, or hold them in the "heart calming" *mudra*: palms up, left hand on top of right with the thumbs touching.

Close your eyes, relax, and take a few deep breaths.

1. Take a long, slow, deep breath, inhaling through the mouth, and imagine that your entire body is filling with bright white light. The light fills every cell in your body, and absorbs all illness, tension, fatigue, and negativity.

2. Exhale in eight short puffs followed by a ninth long puff that extends until your lungs are completely empty. As you exhale, imagine a cloud of dark grey negativity leaving your body and dissolving into nothing.

3. Repeat this inhale-exhale pattern eight times, for a total of nine breaths. I like to visualize the grey exhale becoming lighter with each breath, so by the ninth breath the exhale is clear and clean, and my body is completely free of negativity.

4. Sit quietly for a few moments after you are done, and notice any shifts in your mood and energy.

There are many forms of meditation. Some, like this calming meditation, use specific visualizations. Others teach detached observation of whatever thoughts come up, employ a mantra to focus and still the mind, or simply follow the natural rhythm of the breath. You may want to try a few different approaches before choosing the one that best helps you achieve a calm self-awareness.

I confess that I have been a sporadic meditator for many years and have tried most of the well-known methods, sticking with none of them in spite of my good intentions. About a year ago I was thrilled to discover a high-tech technique that uses sound vibrations to establish a meditative state and support emotional healing. Advanced levels of the program incorporate subliminal affirmations recorded in your own voice. You can find out more by visiting www.centerpointe.com or by calling the Centerpointe Research Institute in Beaverton, OR, at (800) 945-2741.

For more about meditation, see the Resources pages or check out the meditation links at www.fastfengshui.com.

Principle 9

Evaluate Your Results

No one can predict exactly what results you will see from feng shui. The life-shifts you experience may be subtle or dramatic. You may go through a gentle process of empowerment or a real upheaval of the status quo.

Often the effects of feng shui are not exactly what you had in mind. Moving your stuck relationship "forward" may mean breaking up in order that each of you may connect with a more appropriate partner. Improved cash flow may come from an unexpected windfall—or it could result from more clients, a greater workload, and longer hours on the job. Moving ahead in your career might mean *not* getting that promotion, which in turn leads to finding your dream job with another company or in another industry.

You can learn a great deal by examining how you follow through with your feng shui plans, what kinds of results you see, and how you respond to the experience. Feng shui works best when you remain open to a variety of outcomes. Trust that if you have an open heart and a welcoming attitude, the universe will bring you exactly what you need to move you forward on your path.

Quick Tips 106-108 provide suggestions
for how to interpret and learn from your
feng shui experiences.

Quick Tip **106** Embrace change

The single most common barrier to success with feng shui is resistance to change. Achieving our dreams almost always means stretching outside our comfort zone, so it is natural to feel hesitant about what feng shui might bring. Here are three typical situations where resistance to change can prevent feng shui from working. If any of these ring a bell with you, take some time to explore your true readiness for change and your reasons for resisting it.

FEAR OF CHANGE

Every feng shui consultant I know has had the frustrating experience of being hired by a client who resists every suggestion. This inflexibility is a clear indication that the client is not ready for feng shui. If you have read through this book but haven't made any changes yet, what's holding you back? Try making a few minor adjustments first, and hold off on major changes until you are ready.

Sometimes resistance is subconscious—if you've made feng shui adjustments but feel that nothing is working, ask yourself if you are truly ready for what you think you want, and explore whether you might have any hidden resistance that is causing an energetic block.

CLINGING TO THE PAST

Some people turn to feng shui because they want to hold on to things the way they are or to regain something that is slipping away—a job, a relationship, a period when everything seemed to be going just right. Sometimes in these cases there are negative influences in the home that can be corrected through feng shui (Principle 6)—especially if your changed circumstances occurred after moving into a new home. In other cases, however, the bottom line is that life is has moved on and it is time to let go. Feng shui works best when you use it as a tool to move forward in your life, even if that is not an easy transition for you.

RELUCTANCE TO DO THE INNER WORK

Some people hear about the wonderful life changes possible with feng shui, and hope that it can be an easy substitute for therapy. This is rarely effective. Activating your relationship *guas* may provide you with a new opportunity to work through your intimacy issues, but if you cling to the same old patterns and attitudes your new relationship is not likely to be any more successful than the old ones.

Similarly, activating your money *guas* may bring more income, but if you are a compulsive over-spender feng shui won't make you rich—it will just give you more money to throw away.

Instead of hoping for an easy way out, use feng shui as a tool for shifting stuck energy and enhancing your self-awareness, so that you can make the best possible use of whatever coaching or therapy is appropriate for you.

Feng shui has a tendency to bring us those new opportunities and relationships that force us to relinquish old, ineffective behaviors and confront our fears. While this is not always comfortable, it can be powerfully transforming.

Make a commitment to use feng shui as a tool for personal growth, rather than as a quick fix for your problems, and you will inevitably achieve greater success in the long run.

Quick Tip 107 Examine your attitude

When feng shui doesn't work, it is time to see if your attitudes and actions are in line with what you are trying to achieve. Ask yourself: Do I *really* want it? Am I *ready* to receive it? Do I believe I *deserve* it?

Here are some more questions to ask yourself, based on the *gua* or *guas* that you have been working on:

Career .... Do you communicate openly and honestly?
Do you create opportunities for others?
Do your actions demonstrate your abilities?

Self-Understanding .... Do you respect the spiritual beliefs of others?
Do you help others to learn and grow?

Family, Health .... Do you honor your family and friends?
Are you contributing to your community?
Are you a mindful inhabitant of your body?

Money, Prosperity .... Are you generous to others?
Are you a wise caretaker of your assets?

Fame, Reputation) .... Do you recognize others' accomplishments?
Do you refrain from idle or malicious gossip?

Marriage, Romance .... Are you supportive and nurturing to others?
Are you allowing others to nurture you?
Are you comfortable receiving and giving love?

Creativity, Children .... Do you support the creativity of others?
Do you support your children as individuals?

Helpful Friends, Travel .... Are you asking for the help you need?
Are you a benefactor or mentor to others?

Quick Tip **108** Express gratitude

As you learned at the beginning of this book, feng shui is based on the premise that everything is connected energetically, and that our thoughts and intentions are an important factor in the results we see from feng shui. Whatever vibration you project through your thoughts and feelings attracts more of the same energy to you.

It is important to visualize your desired outcome as if it has already happened, because that creates and projects a vibration of joy, satisfaction, and gratitude. Without this important step, it is easy to practice feng shui with our focus fully on what we don't like about our current situation. That creates a vibration of dissatisfaction and lack.

If you vibrate "want," you will keep yourself in a state of wanting. If, on the other hand, you vibrate a joyful "Thank you!," you will attract more experiences to feel thankful about.

In addition to including "as if" visualization in your feng shui empowerment rituals, you can encourage positive benefits from feng shui by shifting your attitude from feeling want for what you don't have to feeling gratitude and thankfulness for all that you have already received. This is not a traditional feng shui teaching, but I believe it is an essential aspect of success with feng shui.

GRATITUDE RITUALS

Here are some suggestions for things you can do to encourage more blessings to flow your way. Choose one of these methods, or make up your own, and practice it at least once a day for 9 or 27 days. First thing in the morning or last thing at night are good times to practice a daily gratitude ritual.

- Make a list of nine or 27 things you are grateful for in your life right now. Keep this list in a red envelope in one of your power spots, under your pillow, or in the *tai chi* (center) of your home. Take it out and read it aloud once a day.

- Make a list every day of nine things you love about yourself or your life. Pay attention to how the list changes over time, and notice how you are opening up and feeling more appreciative of all the blessings in your life.

- Make a list every night of nine nice things that happened to you today. Little things count, like finding your keys in the first place you looked for them, getting to work on time in spite of heavy traffic, a phone call from a friend, or seeing a beautiful blossoming cherry tree beside the road on your way home.

When you look for and focus on the abundance, beauty, and good fortune all around you, you vibrate with joyful appreciation for the generosity and support of the universe, and more blessings and good fortune come your way.

Closing Words

The Fast Feng Shui principles are easy to learn and apply, but that's just the beginning of the feng shui journey. As I'm sure you've noticed by now, my own perspective on feng shui leans heavily toward its use for personal growth and self-discovery. I credit feng shui with enabling me to live a life that a few years ago I had barely dreamed of, and with showing me how much more lies ahead in terms of both personal and professional accomplishments. I hope that, with the help of this book, your experience with feng shui will be as extraordinary and empowering as mine has been.

There is only so much that an author can fit between the covers of a book, and I'm sure some of you have questions that I did not answer here. My website, www.fastfengshui.com, includes a FAQs page of frequently asked questions that you may find helpful. As readers write in with more questions, I will post answers to those as well.

I would love to hear about your successes with feng shui—what issues you had, the problems you identified, and how you used feng shui to correct them. If you learned something new about yourself through feng shui, I'd love to hear about that, too.

One of the things I like best about feng shui is the flexibility it provides for using creative and personal cures and empowerments, so if you've come up with your own quirky ritual or a fun way to activate a power spot, please let me know (and send a photo, if you've got one). I'd also love to see photos of your feng shui collages. Be sure to let me know what you learned or accomplished through that experience, too. If you have an idea for a unique activation or cure, but aren't sure if it's a good one, I'd be happy to offer my opinion. And if you'd just like to share with me what you thought of the book, I want to hear that, too.

You can contact me via the website or by mail at:

Lotus Pond Press
415 Dairy Road, Suite E-144
Kahului, Maui, HI 96732-2398

Resources

IMPORTANT NOTE

The information in this section is highly personal—being based on my own preferences and practice—and is by nature both incomplete and out-of-date. I'm sure it omits many good books, videos, and training programs that I have not yet read, viewed, or experienced, as well as those that become available after this book goes to print.

For a more comprehensive and frequently updated guide to feng shui-related information, I recommend a visit to the extensive "Links & Resources" pages at www.fastfengshui.com.

Books & Videos

TRADITIONAL CHINESE FENG SHUI

If you would like to learn more about the traditional Form, Compass, and Eight Directions methods of feng shui, I recommend:

> Lillian Too, *The Illustrated Encyclopedia of Feng Shui,* Element Books, 2000
>
> Eva Wong, *Feng Shui: The Ancient Wisdom of Harmonious Living for Modern Times,* Shambala, 1996

CONTEMPORARY WESTERN FENG SHUI

I like these for their case-study approach and exquisite photographs:

> R.D. Chin, *Feng Shui Revealed,* Clarkson N. Potter, 1998
>
> Gina Lazenby, *The Feng Shui House Book,* Watson Guptill, 1998

The following titles are among my favorites for beginners:

> Terah Kathryn Collins, *The Western Guide to Feng Shui: Creating Balance, Harmony and Prosperity in Your Environment,* Hay House, 1996
>
> Steven Post, *Modern Feng Shui: Vitality and Harmony for the Home and Office,* Dell, 1998
>
> William Spear, *Feng Shui Made Easy: Designing Your Life with the Ancient Art of Placement,* HarperSanFrancisco, 1995
>
> Angel Thompson, *Feng Shui: how to Achieve the Most Harmonious Arrangement of Your Home and Office,* St. Martin's Griffin, 1996

For an in-depth look at the use of color in feng shui:

> Sarah Rossbach, *Living Color: Master Lin Yun's Guide to Feng Shui and the Art of Color,* Kodasha, 1994

For a holistic approach to home design:

> Robin Lennon, *Home Design from the Inside Out: Feng Shui, Color Therapy, and Self-Awareness,* Penguin USA, 1997

CLUTTER CLEARING

Karen Kingston, *Clear Your Clutter with Feng Shui*, Broadway, 1999

Michelle Passoff, *Lighten Up! Free Yourself from Clutter*, Harper Collins, 1998

VISUALIZATION

Sonia Choquette, *Your Heart's Desire*, Three Rivers Press, 1997

Shakti Gawain, *Creative Visualization*, New World Library, 1995

Lynn Grabhorn, *Excuse Me, Your Life is Waiting*, Hampton Roads, 2000

SPACE CLEARING & SACRED SPACES

Karen Kingston, *Creating Sacred Space with Feng Shui*, Broadway, 1997

Denise Linn, *Space Clearing: How to Purify and Create Harmony in Your Home*, Contemporary Books, 2000

Peg Streep, *Altars Made Easy: A Complete Guide to Creating Your Own Sacred Space*, HarperSanFrancisco, 1997

GARDEN FENG SHUI

Gill Hale, *The Complete Guide to the Feng Shui Garden*, Storey Books, 1998

Nancilee Wydra, *Feng Shui in the Garden*, NTC Contemporary, 1998

AROMATHERAPY, AND FLOWER ESSENCES

Jami Lin, *The Essence of Feng Shui*, Hay House, 1998

Kathy Keville, *Aromatherapy: A Complete Guide to the Healing Art*, Crossing Press, 1995

Jeffrey G. Shapiro, *The Flower Remedy Book*, North Atlantic Books, 1999

JUICE FASTING & CLEANSING

Dr. Richard Anderson, *Cleanse and Purify Thyself* (two volumes, available from www.ariseandshine.com, or by calling 1-800-688-2444)

Steve Meyerowitz, *Juice Fasting and Detoxification*, Sproutman Pub., 1999

Anna Selby, *New Again! The 28 Day Detox Plan*, Ulysses, 1999

Pamela Serure, *30 Days to Vitality: Cleanse Your Body, Clear Your Mind, Claim Your Spirit,* Harper Collins, 1998

TRADITIONAL CHINESE MEDICINE

Harriet Beinfield & Efrem Korngold, *Between Heaven and Earth: A Guide to Chinese Medicine*, Ballantine, 1992

Ted J. Kaputchuk, *The Web That Has No Weaver, Understanding Chinese Medicine*, Contemporary Books, 2000

TAI CHI CHUAN & QIGONG

Books:

Kenneth S. Cohen, *The Way of Qigong: The Art and Science of Chinese Energy Healing*, Ballantine, 1997

Sophia Delza, *Tai Chi Chuan: Body and Mind in Harmony*, SUNY Press, 1986

Bill Douglas, *The Complete Idiot's Guide to Tai Chi and Qigong*, Macmillan, 1998

Roger Jahnke, *The Healer Within*, HarperSanFrancisco, 1999

Videos:

Tai Chi and Qigong: The Prescription for the Future (3 tapes), Bill Douglas

Tai Chi for Health: Yang Long Form, Terence Dunn

Qigong—Awakening & Mastering the Medicine Within You, Roger Jahnke

AYURVEDA

Vasant Lad, *The Complete Book of Ayurvedic Home Remedies*, Three Rivers, 1999

Gopi Warrier & Deepika Gurawat, *The Complete Illustrated Guide to Ayurveda*, Element, 1997

YOGA

Books:

Beryl Bender Birch, *Power Yoga: The Total Strength and Flexibility Workout*, Fireside, 1995; *Beyond Power Yoga: 8 Levels of Practice for Body and Soul*, Fireside, 2000

T.K.V. Desikachar, *The Heart of Yoga: Developing a Personal Practice*, Inner Traditions, 1999

Erich Schiffman, *Yoga: The Spirit and Practice of Moving into Stillness*, Pocket Books, 1996

David Swenson, *Ashtanga Yoga*, Ashtanga Yoga Publications, 1999

Videos (Yoga):

Yoga with Richard Freeman: Ashtanga Yoga, the Primary Series, Delphi Prod.

Ashtanga Yoga Short Forms and *Ashtanga Yoga First Series*, David Swenson

Living Yoga, multiple-tape series produced by Living Arts

MEDITATION, SPIRITUALITY, AND MORE...

Joan Budiliovsky, *The Complete Idiot's Guide to Meditation*, Macmillan, 1998

Dr. Wayne Dyer, *Real Magic: Creating Miracles in Everyday Life*, HarperCollins, 1992

Mark Epstein, *Thoughts Without a Thinker: Psychotherapy from a Buddhist Perspective*, 1995

Shakti Gawain, *The Path of Transformation: How Healing Ourselves can Change the World*, Nataraj, 1993

His Holiness the Dalai Lama and Howard C. Cutler, MD, *The Art of Happiness: A Handbook for Living*, Riverhead Books, 1998

Thich Naht Han, *The Miracle of Mindfulness: A Manual on Meditation*, Beacon Press, 1996

John Wellwood (ed.), *Ordinary Magic: Everyday Life as Spiritual Path*, Shambala, 1992

Machaelle Small Wright, *Behaving as if the God in all Things Mattered*, Perelandra, 1997

Feng Shui Resources

FENG SHUI SUPPLIES

Feng Shui Warehouse; 1-800-388-1599;
www.fengshuiwarehouse.com

Feng Shui Emporium: 1-800-443-5849; www.fengshuiemporium.com

Petals (life-like plants, flowers, and arrangements): 1-800-920-6000;
www.petals.com

FENG SHUI CONSULTANTS

To find a consultant near you, check these on-line directories:

Feng Shui Warehouse: www.fengshuiwarehouse.com

Feng Shui Directory: www.fengshuidirectory.com

Feng Shui Guild: www.fengshuiguild.com

FENG SHUI TRAINING PROGRAMS

The Accelerated Path: (718) 256-2640; www.fengshui-
santopietro.com

BTB Feng Shui Professional Training Program: (415) 681-1182;
www.btbfengshui.org

The Metropolitan Institute of Interior Design: (516) 845-4033;
www.met-design.com

Natural Bridges Institute: (714) 536-2115; www.nbinstitute.com

The Western School of Feng Shui: 1-800-300-6785; www.wsfs.com

Traditional Chinese feng shui and astrology:

American Feng Shui Institute (Larry Sang) www.amfengshui.com

Roger Green (seminars and study tours):
www.fengshuiseminars.com

Joseph Yu (correspondence programs and seminars): www.astro-
fengshui.com .

Glossary

ba gua A map of the energetic qualities of a space. *"Ba gua"* means "eight areas"—eight *guas*, or sections, surround a central space, the *tai chi*. Each *gua* has a symbolic association with a specific life aspect or aspiration, such as wealth, career, or relationships, for example. Whatever is going on energetically in each *gua* of your home will affect the related aspect of your life.

bau-biologie The science of healthy homes. Studies the impact of toxic building materials, electro-magnetic radiation (EMF) and other factors on inhabitants, and recommends ways to create a healthier living and working environment.

Black Sect feng shui A very popular method of feng shui, especially in the U.S., introduced by Professor Thomas Lin Yun. Also called "BTB" (Black Tibetan Buddist) feng shui, this approach aligns the *ba gua* with the entry, rather than to the compass. Black sect feng shui emphasizes the power of intention, and incorporates many "transcendental" cures and rituals.

chakras A system of seven energy centers in the human body, located from the base of the spine to the top of the head. Often used in energy-based healing work.

chi The life force present in all things. The practice of feng shui is based on analysis and correction of the *chi* of a space.

chien The area of the *ba gua* associated with helpful friends and travel. See pages 16 and 176 for the qualities and location of *chien gua*.

Compass school feng shui The traditional Chinese method of feng shui. Analysis and diagnosis of the feng shui of a building is based on its specific compass orientation and the year of construction. More complex and often more difficult to apply than Contemporary Western feng shui.

Contemporary Western feng shui (see also "Black Sect feng shui") I use this as an umbrella term to describe feng shui as it is most often practiced in America today—with the *ba gua* oriented to the doorway instead of to compass directions.

cure An adjustment made with the intention of removing or neutralizing a negative influence or *sha chi*, in order to improve the *chi* of a space. Sometimes also used to refer to feng shui enhancements made to enhance or activate a space, where there is no negative influence to be corrected.

dui The area of the *ba gua* associated with creativity and children. See pages 16 and 174 for the qualities and location of *dui gua*.

earth One of the five elements used in feng shui. See the reference chart on page 30 for a summary of the qualities, shapes, and colors associated with the EARTH element.

empowerment The process of adding the power of your own intention to your feng shui cures and enhancements. Empowering your feng shui changes with the power of body, speech, and mind is thought to dramatically improve the outcome.

enhancement An adjustment made with the intention of improving the *chi* of a space. Faceted crystal balls, water fountains and wind chimes are popular feng shui enhancements. Objects and images that have a strong, positive symbolic meaning for the individual are also effective as enhancements.

extension A part of a room or building that "sticks out" from the rest of the structure and adds strength to that room or *gua*. See page 50 for how to identify any extensions in your home.

Fast Feng Shui™ I created this term to describe my approach to teaching and writing about Contemporary Western feng shui. My emphasis is on: recognizing and working with your feng shui style; targeting your efforts to your individual power spots for maximum results with minimum wasted effort; personalizing the affirmations and visualizations used to empower your changes; the importance of approaching feng shui as tool for change and personal growth.

feng shui The practice, originally from ancient China, of adjusting the *chi*, or life force, of a space so that the inhabitants experience greater happiness, success, prosperity, and vitality.

fire One of the five elements used in feng shui. See the reference chart on page 30 for a summary of the qualities, shapes, and colors associated with the FIRE element.

hsun The area of the *ba gua* associated with money and "fortunate blessings." See pages 16 and 167 for the qualities and location of *hsun gua*.

jen The area of the *ba gua* associated with family and health. See pages 16 and 165 for the qualities and location of *jen gua*.

kan The area of the *ba gua* associated with career. See pages 16 and 161 for the qualities and location of *kan gua*.

karma The fate that you created for yourself in this life as the result of your actions in past lives; the effect that your current actions will have on your future existence.

ken The area of the *ba gua* associated with self-understanding and spirituality. See pages 16 and 163 for the qualities and location of *ken gua*.

kun The area of the *ba gua* associated with marriage and relationships. See pages 16 and 172 for the qualities and location of *kun gua*.

li The area of the *ba gua* associated with fame and reputation. See pages 16 and 170 for the qualities and location of *li gua*.

mantra A sacred word or phrase used for meditation, prayer, and blessing.

metal One of the five elements used in feng shui. See the reference chart on page 30 for a summary of the qualities, shapes, and colors associated with the METAL element.

missing area A part of a room or building that is indented from the rest of the structure and weakens that room or *gua*. See page 51 for how to identify any missing areas in your home.

power spot A focal point for your feng shui efforts. Your personal power spots are determined by what life issues you want to address at this time and by the unique qualities and layout of your home. Feng shui becomes easier and more effective when you concentrate on your power spots first, before working on the rest of your house or apartment.

red envelopes Feng Shui practitioners of the Black Sect or "BTB" school follow the tradition of asking for payment to be presented in red envelopes. The red color empowers the client's wishes and provides protection for the practitioner. Red envelopes can also be used to empower a wish or blessing written on a slip of paper and placed in the envelope.

secret arrows   *Sha* (negative) *chi* created by sharp objects and angles.

sha chi   Harmful *chi* that can cause or aggravate stress, restlessness, and a variety of health problems.

space clearing   Specific rituals and other practices designed to remove stale, old, or negative energy from a space.

tai chi   The central area of any space, especially the center of your home. Anything going on in the *tai chi* of your home will affect all of the *guas*, so it is a very important area to keep free of clutter and other negative influences.

water   One of the five elements used in feng shui. See the reference chart on page 30 for a summary of the qualities, shapes, and colors associated with the WATER element.

wood   One of the five elements used in feng shui. See the reference chart on page 30 for a summary of the qualities, shapes, and colors associated with the WOOD element.

Index

WWW. $\mathcal{F}$ASTFENGSHUI.COM

If you've enjoyed this book, I invite you to explore the many features and resources available online at the Fast Feng Shui website. Here you will find an archive of articles, answers to Frequently Asked Questions about feng shui, free ebooks to download, and of course more titles in the popular Fast Feng Shui series.

You can also subscribe to our free newsletter to receive feng shui tips and advice delivered directly into your in-box twice a month. As a newsletter subscriber you'll get advance notice of new publications and products, as well as special discounts and other offers. As new books, ebooks, and training programs are developed, you'll be the first to hear about them!

Shop our unique collection of handmade feng shui jewelry, crystal bracelets, and jade pendant necklaces—all my original designs—and explore our selection of unusual products and exclusive feng shui gift ideas. Gift certificates are also available for those hard-to-shop-for friends and relatives.

Floor Plan Analysis services and long-distance consultations are also available through the website. And if you're especially interested in finally coping with your clutter, you'll want to visit my clutter site: www.clutterfreeforever.com.

Give the gift
of life transformation and personal growth!

additional copies of

$\mathcal{F}$AST FENG SHUI
9 Simple Principles for
Transforming Your Life by
Energizing Your Home

*can be purchased from
your local independent bookseller
and online at www.fastfengshui.com*

If you wish to pay by personal check, please:

1. Use (or photocopy) the order form on the next page

2. Fill in the information requested

3. Send your order form with payment to the address provided

Yes!

I'd like to order additional copies of

$\mathcal{F}$AST FENG SHUI

9 Simple Principles for Transforming Your Life
by Energizing Your Home

Name: _____

Address:_____

City: _____ State:____ Zip:_____

phone:_____ email:_____

(please provide a telephone number and/or email address
in case we have to contact you about your order)

Please send me:

_____ copies of Fast Feng Shui

_____ copies of Fast Feng Shui for Singles (avail.Dec. 1, 2001)

Enclose $16.95 + $4.95 shipping & handling
for each book ordered.
(Hawaii residents, add $0.91 sales tax per book.)

☐ I'm not ordering at this time, but please let me know
when new Fast Feng Shui™ titles are available!

Mail this form with your check or money order
payable to "Lotus Pond Press" to:

LOTUS POND PRESS
415 Dairy Road, Suite E-144
Kahului, Maui, HI 96732-2398